Romancing Minnesota

Intimate Places
to Stay & Dine

Romancing Minnesota

Intimate Places to Stay & Dine

By Kate Crowley & Mike Link

Pfeifer-Hamilton
Duluth, Minnesota

Pfeifer-Hamilton Publishers
210 West Michigan
Duluth MN 55802-1908 218-727-0500

Romancing Minnesota: Intimate Places to Stay & Dine

Printed in the United States of America by Versa Press Inc.

10 9 8 7 6 5 4 3 2 1

Editorial Director: Susan Gustafson
Manuscript Editor: Tony Dierckins
Art Director: Joy Morgan Dey
Cover Photo: Jay Steinke

Library of Congress Catalog Card Number: 94-74989

ISBN 1-57025-043-X

To our ancestors and the love they shared;

to our children and the love they will find.

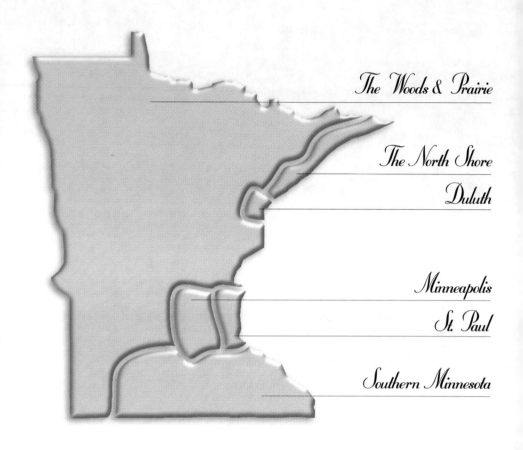

The Woods & Prairie

The North Shore

Duluth

Minneapolis

St. Paul

Southern Minnesota

$\mathcal{M}$innesota has many beautiful and interesting
regions. Select one that you would like to visit,
read about the romantic destinations in that area,
and then choose a spot to share with someone special.

Contents

Places to stay

Places to dine

*We suggest that you call ahead
to verify your accommodations.*

Minneapolis

The Woods & Prairie

Southern Minnesota

The North Shore

xi

Duluth

Introduction

Minnesota is known for many things: Lake Superior's shoreline, majestic forests and prairies, beautiful urban areas, and of course, its many lakes. We think Minnesota is a great place for people in love to enjoy each others' company, so we traveled the state in search of special getaways where couples can rekindle the romance in their relationship.

After visiting countless restaurants, inns, hotels, and bed-and-breakfasts, we present here our favorite romantic retreats from fishing lodges to sophisticated eateries. In their comfortable accommodations and appetizing cuisine, their attentive service and charming details, the establishments discussed within these pages provide an atmosphere that encourages romantic intimacy.

Of course, there's more to romance than candlelight dinners. Throughout the book, we have included suggestions for making Minnesota a place for intimate adventures whether your preference is cross-country skiing or an evening at the opera.

After you've tried some of the places we suggest, create a personal list of your favorite destinations. Take time to visit them often, and you'll keep the spark in your romance for years to come.

We hope you enjoy *Romancing Minnesota* and all the places it takes you.

St. Paul Hot Spots

Uptown

Besides Cafe Latte or W. A. Frost and Company, try a meal at Dixies, Ciatti's, Lotus, La Cucaracha, the Uptowner Diner, Sweeney's, Billy's, or one of the many other fine places to eat and drink near St. Paul's historic Cathedral Hill. But this area offers more than food and beverage. Dozens of unique shops displaying items from books to antiques line either side of Grand Avenue. The magnificent houses of Summit Avenue lie just one block north, and the Cathedral of St. Paul is just a short walk toward downtown. Each spring the area shows off with a parade, live music, food, drink, and sidewalk sales at the annual Grand Old Days celebration.

Landmark Square

With its art displays, the Ordway Theater (perhaps Minnesota's best theater for musical productions), a lovely park, and the St. Paul Hotel (which serves the Twin Cities' best Irish coffee), Landmark Square makes a great place to spend an evening.

Como Park Zoo

Renovated during the 1980s, Como Park Zoo has a new look. Surrounded by rolling hills for picnics, it makes the perfect setting for an afternoon of romance. Couples can have fun watching the animals, enjoy a romantic stroll in the Japanese gardens or Conservatory (the setting for many wedding photos), and end with a picnic by the lake.

Harriet Island and Navy Island

Just next to downtown, on the Mississippi River, Harriet and Navy Islands play host to a number of summertime events, including plenty of live music. The Jonathan Paddleford and Josiah Snelling paddle wheelers dock nearby and offer afternoon and evening cruises on the Big Muddy. They can even be rented for weddings and receptions.

The Parks

Twin Cities residents have been blessed with one of the best urban park systems in the country. Besides Como Park, visit Mounds Park, a historic Native American burial ground overlooking the Mississippi, or Phalen Park and beautiful Lake Phalen. Better yet, spend an afternoon taking a leisurely drive along Lexington, Johnson, Ford, and the other parkways that link the parks together. The Ford Parkway becomes Minnehaha Parkway as you cross the Ford bridge into Minneapolis where more parks await couples out for a day of fun.

Stillwater

A visit to the river town of Stillwater makes a quick escape for Twin Cities residents. Just a short drive east of St. Paul along the Hudson River, Stillwater is the starting point for St. Croix River cruises or scenic drives up the valley to William O'Brien State Park, Marine on the St. Croix, and Taylor's Falls. In the summer, enjoy the Brown Bag Musical Festival or one of the art fairs that line the riverbanks. Stillwater's older brick buildings now include many antique shops, night spots, and restaurants.

Thorwood Historic Inns

ost to an abundance of Victorian homes built by lumber barons, railroad magnates, and river scions at the end of the last century, the historic river town of Hastings sits where the Mississippi meets the St. Croix River, just a half-hour drive from the Twin Cities. Two of these houses, Thorwood and Rosewood, have been converted into charming bed-and-breakfasts by the owners, Pam and Dick Thorson.

Lumber Baron William Thompson built Thorwood in the late 1890s using white pine rafted down the St. Croix from Minnesota's northern forests. Although it has seen many changes over the past one hundred years, Thorwood remains a fine example of French Second Empire architecture. The tall brick exterior topped by a mansard roof with wide overhangs typifies an architectural style that was popular in the United States during the 1840s and 50s. Queen Ann style also influenced the structure's elegant design.

When the lumber boom died out, the original owner

went into banking. His daughters inherited the home upon his death; they died without heirs and the property passed from the family's hands. In the 1930s it became a hospital. Along with making necessary structural changes, the hospital builders removed many of the ornamental details and decorations. In 1952, new owners converted the house into a six-unit apartment building, removing walls and doors.

The Thorsons bought the house in 1978 with the goal of restoring and preserving it, an immense task. Years of neglect had led to the deterioration of plaster, and the original wood had rotted. In 1980 they moved into the house and began a thorough restoration. In 1983 they opened Thorwood as an inn on a very small scale, but it took another two years before they were ready to expand the room offerings.

With its three levels and bed in a loft, complete with a skylight for nighttime stargazing, Sara's Suite offers Thorwood's perfect escape for a romantic weekend for two.

Their attention to detail and hard work has paid off in a very attractive and comfortable inn. A country style decorates most of the seven guest rooms at Thorwood; some are light and bright, while others have darker-colored walls with light accents in the furnishings. The eleven-foot-high ceilings, typical of the house's era, give the rooms an airy, open feeling. Teddy bears and rag dolls sit on beds and hide in the rooms' many nooks and crannies, adding a whimsical atmosphere to the house.

Four of the rooms are suites, three of which have fireplaces; four of the seven have whirlpools. One room is on the first floor; the others lie up a steep and narrow stair-case. With its three levels and bed in a loft, complete with a skylight for nighttime stargazing, Sara's Suite offers Thorwood's perfect escape for a romantic weekend for two.

While Thorwood is located in the northwest section of town, Rosewood rests in the east, just two blocks from Hasting's historic downtown area. The inn offers guests their choice of eight rooms; seven have whirlpools, all but one have fireplaces, and one unique room occupies a four-season porch. An emphasis on lace, flowers, and brass beds runs throughout the inn. The three suites on the top floor cover 1,200 square feet illuminated by

If you wish, you can enjoy breakfast in the main floor's formal dining room, but not many guests can pass up a breakfast picnic in bed.

six skylights and several other windows of unusual shape.

Guests at both inns receive a lovely snack basket soon after arrival. The wicker containers hold an assortment of fruit, bread, crackers, and cheese. These same baskets bring breakfast to your door at whatever hour of the morning you desire; two are needed to carry all their appetizing contents. One contains juice, coffee, and/or tea, a morning paper, and a single rose; the other holds warm, freshly baked sweet rolls or muffins, a fruit plate with sweet yogurt topping, sausage or bacon, and eggs prepared in your choice of a variety of ways. If you wish, you can enjoy breakfast in the main floor's formal dining room, but not many guests pass up a breakfast picnic in bed.

For evening meals, guests have several dinner options at the inns, or you can drive into town and eat at the Mississippi Belle or cross the river to the Steamboat Inn in Prescott, Wisconsin. In fact, while it's tempting to spend your entire time in the inns' very comfortable surroundings, Hastings offers a wide variety of interesting places to visit and things to do.

Listed on the National Register of Historic Places, downtown Hastings has been preserved as an example of a nineteenth-century main street. Since many of its Victorian homes feature front porches, the town holds a special Front Porch Festival every year during the last weekend of May. This gives visitors and townspeople an excuse to wander the neighborhoods, admiring the architecture. Rivertown Days in mid-July offers water shows, entertainment, races, arts and crafts, food and music, a lighted boat parade, and fireworks, all designed to focus attention on the Mississippi River.

No matter how you choose to spend your stay at Thorwood or Rosewood, Pam and Dick will make certain that you are comfortable and satisfied. Both enjoy talking with their guests and sharing information about the area and the history of both inns. If honeymooners and guests celebrating

50 Ways to **Lure your Lover**

If you have chosen a Victorian mansion for your stay, step back in time and dress the part.

anniversaries let the proprietors know of the occasion in advance, some special touches will be added to your visit. Both inns have a no smoking policy, so smokers must use the porches or stroll the grounds. Visitors should also be aware that the inns' have a two-night minimum stay on weekends.

Hastings is hometown for the cartoon characters and toys, Gumby and Pokey. They got their start in this town in 1966.

THORWOOD • 315 PINE STREET • HASTINGS

ROSEWOOD • 620 RAMSEY STREET • HASTINGS

612-437-3297 • 800-992-INNS

STEAMBOAT CRUISES, ST. PAUL TO GALENA, ILLINOIS

THEME CRUISES FOR DIFFERENT SEASONS

Mississippi Queen Steamboat

Many a young mind has been stirred by the romance of Mississippi River life through the tales of Mark Twain. The author—who took his pen name from a riverboat navigational term used when determining water depth—has become synonymous with the wide, lazy river and the grand steamboats that once graced its waters. His stories of Huck Finn and Tom Sawyer fill our minds with visions of freedom and escape.

The Delta Queen Steamboat Company offers modern-day river enthusiasts a chance to relive the glorious days Twain portrayed in his work, days when steamboat paddle wheelers offered a more sociable, sedate mode of transportation. Its *Mississippi Queen* steamboat has brought passengers up and down the Big Muddy and in and out of the past since 1976. During the summer and into fall, cruises on the riverboat originate in downtown St. Paul and head south to Galena, Illinois, before returning to Minnesota.

Built in 1976, the *Mississippi Queen* is the world's

largest, most luxurious steamboat. At 382 feet long and 68 feet wide, she would dwarf the grandest paddle wheelers that plied American rivers a century ago, when they ruled the waterways. Glittering, garnished, and shining bright white, the *Mississippi Queen* resembles a floating, five-tiered wedding cake.

Victorian elegance and modern comfort and convenience combine to make a cruise on the *Queen* a trip couples won't soon forget. Decorated with plaster moldings, bas-relief ceilings, Victorian valances, wing chairs, and sofas, its various lounges and salons harken back to earlier eras. A gleaming brass three-story grand staircase beckons passengers to the upper decks, while elevators provide an alternative for those who can't manage stairs or who simply prefer to admire the staircase as they rest their legs.

Victorian elegance combined with modern comfort and convenience make a cruise on the Queen a trip couples won't soon forget.

The second, or Texas deck, features the grand saloon, richly furnished with cushioned white wicker furnishings patterned after the "ladies' lounges" of nineteenth-century steamboats. Covering nearly half the length of the boat, the saloon serves as a lecture hall, informal dining area, and comfortable conversation and game parlor during the daylight hours. At night it is transformed into a concert hall and ballroom.

Opposite the grand saloon on the Texas deck is the dining saloon, another grand room elegantly decorated with crystal chandeliers and so many brass surfaces and mirrors that everything sparkles and glows with a warm, golden light. As with all cruises, guests enjoy the same table and attentive servers during the entire cruise, creating a friendly atmosphere that adds sincerity to their singing "Happy Birthday" or "Happy Anniversary." Guests have a variety of meal options, including full meals, happy-hour snacks, midmorning coffee breaks, midafternoon teas, and a late night buffet. Of course, those who feel a little peckish between meals can get nibbles at one of the bars.

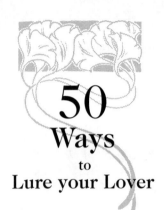

**50
Ways**
to
Lure your Lover

Watch for eagles,

tundra swans,

and peregrine

falcons as you

travel along

the river.

Accommodations range from expensive, spacious upper-deck suites to cozy below-deck cabins. Midrange staterooms complete with outside decks offering a view of the river line both sides of the boat. Each cabin comes equipped with a small bathroom and shower, but some below deck cabins have no windows. The deluxe suites also come with a bathtub. Visitors used to large hotel rooms common in the United States may be surprised at the *Queen's* compact rooms, a feature also standard on board all oceangoing cruise ships. But the rooms are neat and clean and include hotel services such as fresh toiletries, a constant supply of ice, and beds turned down each night, their pillows harboring a good-night treat.

The Minnesota to Illinois tour is especially popular

in the fall when the hardwood forests lining both sides of the river burst into shades of burgundy, ocher, rust, and cinnamon. You can see the progression of color as you travel south into warmer regions. Summertime tours offer an opportunity to soak up sunshine and that lazy "Ol' Man River" atmosphere.

Whatever season you choose, keep in mind the words of a captain on the earlier paddle wheeler *Gordon C. Green* as he described past river journeys on his boat: "She disconnected herself from civilization every time her planks were hauled in and went away into a dream world of her own making."

Renew your wedding vows on board. The captain performs a special ceremony on every cruise, complete with photographs and certificates.

If you like to listen to classical or modern jazz and pop music, we suggest you bring along a portable tape or CD player. There is a two-channel radio in each room, but its offerings tend to be Dixieland, early 50s, swing, ragtime, and Rogers and Hammerstein.

> *Have coffee delivered to your room at*
> *daybreak so you can watch the sunrise*
> *over the Mississippi's wooded bluffs from*
> *the privacy and comfort of your bed.*

THE DELTA QUEEN STEAMBOAT CO.

800-543-7637 FOR INFORMATION

800-543-1949 FOR RESERVATIONS

STILLWATER
ELEGANT GUEST ROOMS
GRACIOUS DINING

Lowell Inn

nown as the "Mount Vernon of the West," the Lowell Inn has offered guests a romantic location to stay and dine since 1930. The colonial architecture that gives the inn its nickname features a red brick exterior and thirteen white pillars gracing the front veranda. The inn rests on a quiet street in Stillwater, just a few blocks up from the banks of the St. Croix River. The luxurious inn's lobby, dining rooms, and guest rooms leave visitors with a feeling of an earlier, more sedate and dignified era.

Arthur Palmer, Jr., and his wife, Maureen, the current innkeepers, continue the tradition of gracious hospitality begun with Arthur's parents, Nell and Arthur, Sr. Art and Nell shared a great fondness for French Provincial and Victorian furnishings, and over the years they collected a vast assortment of artwork and practical pieces for their dining and guest rooms. The last reconstruction and remodeling of the inn's twenty-one rooms began in 1973 and took eight years to complete.

Today, when most inns and bed-and-breakfasts reflect a country or Victorian style, the Lowell Inn remains distinct with its emphasis on baroque and rococo detailing. Here guests find gilt edging and crystal lighting fixtures, as well as lacy curtains and satin bedspreads in the guest rooms. They also find a cat lounging on the bed, but these cats do not move or purr; they are porcelain mascots, for decoration only. Six rooms were given new baths during the last renovation. Unique in their opulence, some of the new baths feature in-the-round showers and jacuzzis, fluted and scalloped marble sinks with gold plated faucets, and toilets that very much resemble thrones.

Although its rooms are gracious and elegant, the inn's best feature is its three dining rooms, each offering guests a unique dining atmosphere and experience.

Although its rooms are gracious and elegant, the inn's best feature is its three dining rooms, each offering guests a unique dining atmosphere and experience. Sheffield silver services, Dresden china collections, pastel-colored sandwich glass, and Irish linen embellish the George Washington Room, and heavy drapes flank its long oval windows as portraits of George and Martha gaze out at diners. This very formal room features Williamsburg service by the staff. They present food, offer choices, and, after you've selected, place individual portions on your plate. A server holds the relish tray as you pick what you'd like. In today's world of fast food and casual dining, formal dining such as this might feel somewhat awkward, but the inn's friendly and patient

15

servers make it a comfortable, enjoyable experience for all.

Like an indoor arbor, the Garden Room allows visitors to enjoy the beauty of Minnesota's forests and streams even during the coldest winter nights. In the center of the room a natural spring bubbles up into a rock pool holding trout that diners can choose for their meal. The sound of flowing water, the green color scheme, and polished agate tables make diners feel hidden in a bower.

Next door to the Garden Room, the Matterhorn Room, established after Art and Maureen visited Switzerland in search of their ancestral roots, awaits guests with a taste for Alpine cuisine. Impressed by the exquisite wood carvings they found on their tour, the Palmers decided to decorate the third dining room using this artwork. Its dark wood paneling and beams and acid-etched stained glass windows create a highly intimate setting, where conversation in the glow of warm yellow light casts a romantic spell.

A meal in the Matterhorn Room offers a simple yet unique and delightful experience influenced by the Palmers' Swiss heritage. The menu includes escargot sauteed in a secret seasoning, a special lettuce salad, and Fondu Bourguignone, beef cooked in natural oils and dipped in a variety of

**50
Ways**
to
Lure your Lover

*Attend
Stillwater's
Brown Bag
Festival. Pack a
champagne
lunch to share
in a secluded
spot along the
Mississippi.*

special sauces. Dessert consists of Grapes Florentine or Devonshire, and a four-course wine service accompanies each meal. The lingering dining experience gives guests a sense of Old World charm and excellence.

The Lowell Inn bears itself proudly, as an elegant, aging aristocrat should—a little frayed at the edges, but always gracious and thoroughly dignified.

The Lowell Inn encourages elegance. Dress to the hilt, live it up, be formal; enjoy the service, the garnishes, the great wine list, the Brandy Alexanders. Go first class.

102 N. 2ND ST. • STILLWATER

612-439-1100

OPEN YEAR ROUND

17

SOUTHWEST ST. PAUL

MIDDLE EASTERN CUISINE

TRADITIONAL MUSIC AND DANCE

Caravan Serai

ust over the Ford bridge from Minneapolis, the white stucco facade of Caravan Serai restaurant hides among frequently vacant storefronts across the parkway from the Ford plant. Adventurous diners who wander in from this not-too-romantic location will be pleased as they find themselves swept into another world, where the air is filled with Middle Eastern music and the scents of exotic spices and herbs.

The oldest Afghan restaurant in the United States, Caravan Serai was established by Abdul Kayoum in 1971. With family ties to Afghani royalty, Abdul grew up attending feasts at the palace and developed a taste for the finest foods. His mother, cousin to King Zahir Shah, often hired chefs who had worked for the king. Abdul spent many hours in the kitchen watching the chefs prepare the specialities of the country, and he and other family members brought many of the recipes to the United States. Together with excellent service, these recipes guarantee patrons of Caravan Serai true royal treatment. Caravan Serai is currently owned and managed by Abdul's daughter Nancy and her husband, Gregory Stevens. The two have incorporated foods and decor from northern India and other Middle Eastern countries, but the restaurant's Afghan origins remain at the center of the menu.

The oldest Afghan restaurant in the United States, Caravan Serai transports diners into the world of Arabian nights, casbahs, and bazaars.

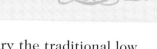

With three dining rooms—one with standard tables and chairs and two with low tables and round black naugahyde pillows—Caravan Serai offers accommodations for families or a romantic night out. Couples must try the traditional low tables, the inspiration for Caravan Serai's motto, "The Best Restaurant in Town for Pillow Talk."

Draped tent-like fabric covers the ceilings, creating an exotic atmosphere that transports diners out of the mundane Midwest and into the world of Arabian nights, casbahs, and bazaars. On the walls hang ornate woven camel saddlebags, large brass serving trays, and a tapestry depicting a princess being carried off on horseback by Moorish warriors. The glass-topped tables rest on silk Indian sari cloth with metallic threads that glitter in the low lights.

Diners unfamiliar with Middle Eastern fare will appreciate the menu's delicious descriptions of each entree, complete with an indication of its country or region of origin. Fresh vegetables accompany each meal, along with a choice of soup or salad, rice, and the special bread used to dip hummus, a rich blend of chick peas, sesame paste, and spices. Lamb, the traditional meat of Afghan cooking, is available in four or five entrees, and beef and chicken dishes are livened with curry, ginger, garlic, or cucumber sauce. A selection of four vegetarian entrees complements the menu, and three standard American entrees await the more timid diner.

Those tempted by several entrees can satisfy their appetites with the Ghengis Kahn Platter, selecting three of the menu's many entrees, accompanied by the traditional side dishes. With the addition of an appetizer, the Ghengis Khan Platter is more than enough to fill the stomachs of couples who like to share. In fact, all servings at Caravan Serai are substantial, and if you find yourself unable to finish, don't worry. A traditional Afghan phrase, "The shame of the plate," implies that diners who did not leave something on their plates were not satisfied, while those with a few bites remaining left the table full.

Saying "I love you"
TURKISH
Seni Seviyorum

Desserts made fresh daily include traditional Middle Eastern sweets with an Afghani flavor. The Sheer Chai—a hot, sweet tea, flavored with cardamom and topped with whipped cream—is a dessert in itself.

While exotic tastes please your palate, traditional music and dance entertain your eyes and ears. One night a week, a guitarist plays; a drummer performs on another. Weekends feature the sensual grace and charm of traditional belly dance. This ancient art mesmerizes both men and women with sinuous movements to the exciting beat of the music, adding to the romantic air of the restaurant. One patron incorporated the belly dancer into his marriage proposal. The dancer entered the darkened dining room carrying a tray of lighted candles on her head and a candle in each hand. As the dance neared its conclusion, she moved close to the couple's table and slowly lowered herself, presenting the tray to the groom-to-be. He picked up a ring that lay hidden among the candles and handed it to his beloved. The fully packed restaurant burst into applause as she emotionally accepted his proposal.

2175 FORD PARKWAY • ST. PAUL

612-690-1935

HOURS: TUESDAY–FRIDAY, 11:00 A.M.–2:00 P.M.

SUNDAY–THURSDAY, 5:00 P.M.–9:30 P.M.

FRIDAY–SATURDAY, 5:00 P.M.–10:30 P.M.

CLOSED ON EASTER, THANKSGIVING, AND CHRISTMAS

LOCATED ON HISTORIC CATHEDRAL HILL
VICTORIAN RESTAURANT
INTIMATE, ELEGANT, OR OUTDOOR DINING

W. A. Frost and Company

From the time it was built in the late 1890s until the end of the 1930s, W. A. Frost's Pharmacy enjoyed a prosperous business in the heart of St. Paul's fashionable Cathedral Hill District. Unfortunately, the neighborhood, with its elegant Victorian homes and buildings, fell into decline. In the 1970s, however, a resurgence of interest in the Cathedral Hill District and its valuable houses and business structures brought investment and renovation to the area. In 1975 W. A. Frost and Company opened its doors once again, this time as a restaurant. For many years it was a well-guarded secret for patrons who cherished its intimate and easy atmosphere, but inevitably the beautiful eatery's reputation spread.

Custom made for romantics, a Victorian flavor permeates the restaurant's decor. The ceilings are fitted with pressed and painted tin, and the original tin work still hangs over the bar. Dark florals paper some of the walls, while other walls of exposed brick, display huge oil paintings from the nineteenth and early twentieth centuries. Diners enjoy a natural separation of tables in rooms of varying size, and stained glass doors can be closed to make them more intimate. Large brick fireplaces grace two of the dining rooms, with marble-topped tables arranged near the hearths for couples. Bentwood chairs, pink napkins, and small vases with fresh posies all contribute to the Victorian feeling, and large Oriental rugs cover the hardwood floors, providing a cushion and absorbing sounds. Large windows filter in sunlight to brighten the rooms during the day, and when darkness falls the panes reflect the soft glow of candles and flames in the fireplaces.

While the cave offers a cozy spot for a romantic meal, W. A. Frost's large brick patio is ideal for alfresco dining and relaxed conversation.

Diners of a particularly romantic nature should remember to try the "cave," a secluded dining space set into a rough stone alcove in the basement level. Strings of tiny white lights sparkle on the walls, and pots of artificial geraniums add splashes of color to the nook. Request this perfect spot for a romantic rendezvous in advance to ensure the table is prepared. It is normally used by people who carry their food and drink from the bar.

While the cave offers a cozy spot for a romantic meal, Frost's large brick patio is ideal for alfresco dining and relaxed conversation. On this shaded bi-level terrace, light filters in lacy patterns through the locust trees. In the evening, colored electric lanterns hung among the branches, combine with candles on each table to illuminate the dining area. The grapevines that cover the brick facade of the Dakotah building next to the patio, along with its green and white striped awnings and projecting iron balconies, give patrons the feeling of dining in Paris or possibly New Orleans, especially in the summer when the greenery is lush. But this patio does not close when the leaves fall. The management will serve on the patio as long as people choose to sit outside and the snow doesn't get too deep.

W. A. Frost features separate menus and kitchens for the patio and the interior restaurant, with light continental selections including several types of pasta, grilled pork chops, shrimp, chicken, and a few fish and beef entrees. Nantucket chicken breast, a favorite among patrons, comes stuffed with herb cheese and sits on a bed of tomato sauce topped with a white wine chive cream sauce; and the beef and spinach cannelloni is also served with both red and white sauce.

While W. A. Frost's entrees are guaranteed to please, many regular customers come solely for the salads. A smoked turkey and wild rice salad with pecans and grapes and sherried-mayonnaise dressing has graced the menu for years, and the Szechwan chicken salad features poached chicken and fresh vegetables on a bed

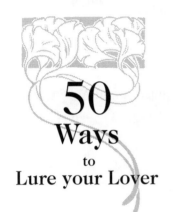

**50
Ways**
to
Lure your Lover

Start a calendar

of your special

days. Lovers

have many

sentimental

occasions to

remember—

celebrate them

annually.

of shredded Napa cabbage topped with peanuts and served with a ginger-garlic dressing. Desserts—in particular the chocolate silk pie, which is as rich and smooth as its name implies—are also a favorite item among W. A. Frost regulars, many of whom stop by just to order the pie and one of the espressos.

The bar at W. A. Frost offers an extensive list of beers, wines, and after-dinner drinks. As many as twenty different wines are available by the glass, though on a hot summer day lazing on the patio, you may prefer to choose one of their eighteen cold specialty drinks. The only difficulty comes in trying to choose just one, since they all have tempting titles and ingredients. The biannual Summit Avenue House Tour in the spring and fall provides an excellent opportunity to try the drinks at Frost's bar, as the tour ends with a complimentary beverage at the historic restaurant. We expect your visit will be the beginning of a long friendship.

On Valentine's Day at W. A. Frost, candy hearts with messages fill dishes placed on each table. Informed in advance of a planned proposal, the staff once filled the dish destined for the couple-to-be's table only with hearts that said "yes."

From F. Scott Fitzgerald to Garrison Keillor,
authors, those most hopeless of romantics,
have been attracted to W. A. Frost.

*When it was a pharmacy, an eccentric
socialite appeared at W. A. Frost's every
afternoon at the same time, dressed all in
black astride her pure white horse. She
would stop at the corner of Selby and
Western and druggist and proprietor
Mr. W. A. Frost would meet her, a glass
of soda in his hand—for the horse.*

SELBY AND WESTERN • ST. PAUL

612-224-5715

HOURS: MONDAY–SATURDAY, 11:00 A.M.–MIDNIGHT

SUNDAY, 10:30 A.M.–11:00 P.M.

CLOSED ON ALL MAJOR HOLIDAYS

REVOLVING RESTAURANT ATOP THE ST. PAUL RADISSON

ROMANTIC PIANO MUSIC

Carousel

An elevator ride overlooking the Mississippi carries couples to Carousel, a restaurant high atop the Radisson Hotel in the heart of downtown St. Paul that promotes and encourages romance. Once inside, diners may sit at tables near the ceiling-high windows on the stationary main floor or ride on the revolving, elevated platform, which completes a full rotation every forty-five minutes.

This carousel for grown-ups has only three horses mounted on the low wall surrounding the dining area, but the romantic fun of the restaurant does not rely on a carnival atmosphere. Recent renovations have opened up the dining space and created a crisp, sleek style for the 90s. The lighting is low and warm, accenting the room's decor, keyed to a soothing, smoky lavender and dark blue-gray carpeting. The restaurant can accommodate many couples, but its arrangement eliminates any feeling of crowding, and the acoustics encourage intimate conversation. A pianist serenades diners for most of the evening.

Arrive at Carousel just before dusk for a sunset view of the river and the surrounding city.

Arrive at Carousel just before dusk for a sunset view of the river and surrounding city. You can watch jets approaching the international airport or small planes taking off at nearby Holman Field, and on clear days the Minneapolis skyline comes into view. Down below, trains run alongside the river, and when the season is right, vessels from houseboats to rowing scows, barges to paddle wheelers ply the waters of the Mississippi. But the real treat is to watch the daylight slip away and the lights begin to spread across the city, creating a European atmosphere as the cathedral rests in silhouette against a blazing orange sky on the western horizon.

While all seats in the restaurant enjoy a marvelous view, tables 20 and 120, set in corners with windows on both sides, provide the best seats for the evening light show. The carousel holds just fifteen tables, so when you call for reservations make sure to request the location you want.

The menu at Carousel offers American cuisine with a flair for the creative, incorporating special flavors and ethnic traditions representative of the many cultures that settled this country. The menu alternates seasonally, and a small group of appetizers, entrees, and desserts change twice a week. The kitchen uses the freshest ingredients available both locally and beyond, including a wonderful choice of seafood.

The chef's specials may include New Zealand red venison, grilled buffalo rib eye, or Great Lakes trout. The restaurant is well known for its prime rib, and even the smaller portion at Carousel fills the hungry diner. Bread, including sourdough French bread or a seven-grain loaf, arrives warm at the table along with the salad. While it's delicious, diners should exercise restraint with the bread or risk finding themselves too full for dessert, a most unfortunate predicament indeed.

Desserts include bananas foster and cherries jubilee, prepared at your table with the traditional flaming of the sauce, a service very few restaurants still offer. Several dessert coffees featuring liqueurs are also served with the flare of the flame, or guests can savor their desserts with a variety of excellent coffees.

Carousel continues to maintain its reputation as a formal restaurant with a relaxed setting and atmosphere (coat and tie are optional). To better serve their customers, they have added a pre-theater dinner menu available from 5:30 to 7 P.M., a post-theater menu served from 10 to 11 P.M., and a special limousine package that includes dinner for two, champagne, dessert, and a limo ride to the restaurant and back after the show.

If you'd prefer to dine at Carousel in daylight, a special Jazz Brunch is served every Sunday.

If you'd prefer to dine at Carousel in daylight, a special Jazz Brunch is served every Sunday from 11 A.M. to 2 P.M. Entrees include familiar egg and meat dishes and special entrees such as blackened chicken breasts, eggs hussard, jambalaya, and a chef-attended Louisiana egg station. Champagne, orange juice, French beignets, hot

50 Ways
to
Lure your Lover

Stroll together

through St. Paul's

Como Park

Conservatory.

Have your picture

taken by the

waterfall, where

many wedding

photos have

been posed.

biscuits, and corn muffins are also included, creating a Dixieland feast along the Mississippi River when New Orleans is just too far to drive.

The romance of revolving high atop Minnesota's capital city has played inspiration to many a wedding proposal. One man brought his date in late in the evening when most of the guests had departed so he could sing to his future fiancée. Another man asked that a dozen roses in an Italian vase be delivered to the table with the appetizers; a card contained his proposal. One creative young man visited the restaurant well before his reservation and provided the chef with matching plates, one with his proposal written on it. Later, his date picked at her vegetable as the nervous groom-to-be waited for her to expose the message. Suddenly she began pushing the food around with her fork and moving her face closer to the plate; a broad smile formed, and the young man handed her the box with the ring. Others have placed an engagement ring in a sugar bowl, a champagne glass, or a dessert dish, on top of the ice cream, and even in the center of a tomato cut into the shape of a rose. Many people who became engaged at the Carousel or shared their first date there return on anniversaries and request the same table.

22ND FLOOR • RADISSON HOTEL

11 E. KELLOGG BLVD. • ST.PAUL

612-292-0408

HOURS: MONDAY–THURSDAY, 6:30 A.M.–10:30 P.M.

FRIDAY, 6:30 A.M.–11:30 P.M.

SATURDAY, 7:00 A.M.–11:30 P.M.

SUNDAY, 7:00 A.M.–10:30 P.M.

OPEN 365 DAYS A YEAR

GRAND AVENUE
CAFETERIA-STYLE BISTRO

Cafe Latté

ost diners might consider a busy restaurant with cafeteria-style self-service an unromantic spot for a romantic outing, but they will find an evening or afternoon at the Cafe Latté quite to the contrary. Full of life, the cafe offers the festive air of an off-Broadway bistro, where people come to see and be seen —the perfect spot to begin or end a night that includes the theater.

The interior of the restaurant gleams with chrome and glass counters, tables, stairways, and a full wall of windows. With two levels of dining space to choose from, customers easily find a good view of the colorful passing parade outside.

As they first enter the slow-moving line, guests are tempted with a decadent display of chocolate tortes, creamy cheesecakes, and other rich desserts. Moving along, the options turn to delicious sandwiches made with freshly baked breads and packed full of meats, avocados, sprouts, tomatoes, and a variety of spreads. Their salad selection far surpasses what most other restaurants offer. Down the line, guests encounter a fine selection of soups thick and full of rich flavors, including an incredible chicken salsa chili, wonderfully hot and tasty and topped with sour cream, onions, cheese, and nachos.

Eventually, diners come upon the coffees for which the restaurant is named. The Midwest offers no better cappuccinos, espressos, or lattes than those found here. Those who don't want caffeine can try the "Moos," hot milk drinks with a choice of chocolate, almond, and other flavorings, topped with thick whipped cream. Beer, wine, juice, and soda are also available.

50
Ways
to
Lure your Lover

Go to an antiquarian bookstore and find an old magazine from the year you were married or started dating. Spend the evening reminiscing over coffee or wine on your life together.

850 GRAND AVE. • ST. PAUL

612-224-5687

HOURS: MONDAY–THURSDAY, 9:00 A.M.–11:00 P.M.

FRIDAY, 9:00 A.M.–MIDNIGHT

SATURDAY, 8:00 A.M.–MIDNIGHT

SUNDAY, 8:00 A.M.–10:00 P.M.

NO RESERVATIONS NECESSARY

ST. PAUL'S HISTORIC LOWER TOWN
MINNEAPOLIS AND ST. PAUL LOCATIONS
ORIGINAL THAI CUISINE

Sawatdee Thai

alled the Land of Smiles, Thailand is home to a friendly, gracious people anxious to see smiles on their visitor's faces. In this land of great beauty, the word *sawatdee* acts as both a warm greeting and a fond farewell. The term also helps form the names of the Twin Cities' two finest Thai restaurants, owned and operated by a pair of sisters from Thailand. While both eateries have similar menus and provide the same friendly service, the distinct personality of each sister shows in some of the special events the restaurants host throughout the year.

The Thai New Year, probably the most popular and colorful celebration, occurs in April. In the St. Paul restaurant, a somewhat sedate celebration presents Thai folk dance and music along with a traditional water blessing of all guests. The celebration in Minneapolis also features song and dance, but often includes a demonstration of kick boxing, a costume contest, and Thai games that bring much laughter to the audience and participants alike. The owner, an ebullient entertainer, likes to take over as master of ceremonies, and Minneapolis patrons find the water blessing a little more damp than the one at the St. Paul site.

While the traditions of Thailand create an enchanting evening for couples, its food guarantees a smile on the faces of all guests. Borrowing some of the qualities of Chinese, Indian, and Malaysian cooking, Thai food creates its own unique and delicious style and flavors. The delectable blending results in food that can become almost addictive. The grand buffet offered at each Sawatdee restaurant allows guests to sample a variety of dishes, sweet, sour, salty, tangy, hot, and very hot.

50
Ways
to
Lure your Lover

Eat at an ethnic restaurant, then spend the evening planning a dream trip together.

289 EAST 5TH ST. • ST.PAUL

612-222-5859

607 WASHINGTON AVE. SO. • MINNEAPOLIS

612-338-6451

HOURS: SUNDAY–THURSDAY, 11:00 A.M.–10:00 P.M.

FRIDAY AND SATURDAY, 11:00 A.M.–11:00 P.M.

Additional Restaurants

*Couples out for dinner in the St. Paul
area might also try one of these
fine establishments.*

The Dakota

1021 BANDANA BOULEVARD EAST, BANDANA SQUARE • ST. PAUL

612-642-1442

If you like the mood of an intimate jazz club, with music surrounding your table and the feeling that the musicians play just for you and your date, this is the place. The Dakota attracts the top names in jazz while bringing a 1990s touch to an old tradition. Concentrating on Midwest cuisine, the restaurant serves food raised in the area but prepared with a flair as creative as the jazz notes floating through the dining room. The bar is spacious and well stocked with all the traditional liquors as well as specialties.

Dock Cafe

425 EAST NELSON ST. • STILLWATER

612-430-3770

Located off the main street and a block downstream from the St. Croix River bridge, Stillwater's Dock Cafe offers river viewing, relaxation, and a perfect place to get away from the bustle of this river town's festive shops and waterfront. Even when the weather is too cold for diners to enjoy the patio, the dining room's glassed-in fireplace makes a cozy focus for wintertime dining. The bakery's sourdough—their specialty—garnishes most offerings. Both regional and world-influenced, the eclectic menu, which includes Caribbean chicken wings, gravlax (Norwegian cured salmon), Star Prairie smoked trout, Madeira chicken, and veal Garibaldi defies categorization.

The St. Paul Grill

350 MARKET ST. • WITHIN THE ST. PAUL HOTEL • ST. PAUL

612-224-7455

On the main floor of the St. Paul Hotel, this upscale restaurant and lounge makes a perfect stop for couples on their way to or from the Ordway Theatre, Landmark Center, the St. Paul Auditorium, the library, and Rice Park. The bar serves the city's best Irish Coffee (as attested to by at least one Irish visitor) and presents a good wine and single malt scotch list.

Minneapolis Hot Spots

The Parks

The City of Lakes matches its twin to the east with its own set of wonderful parks centered around its lakes. Near Uptown in South Minneapolis, three lakes—Calhoun, Harriet, and Lake of the Isles—connected by streams and pathways, make wonderful spots for a romantic stroll, bike ride, canoe ride, or swim. Pause to enjoy Lake Harriet's Rose Garden, which is fragrant with flowers through most of the summer. Minnehaha Falls with its legend of long-ago lovers may inspire poetic words from modern-day couples.

The Warehouse District

The Target Center is surrounded by opportunities for downtown dining, drinking, and socializing. Besides Cafe Brenda and Chez Bananas, try The Loon, Pickled Parrot, Chicago Grill, The Fine Line, Lion's Pub, Urban Wildlife, Rosen's, or any of the dozens of other establishments offering everything from a fun night of dancing to a quiet, romantic meal.

Seven Corners

With Dudley Riggs' theater on one side, Theatre in the Round on the other, and Grandma's, Bullwinkles, and Sergeant Preston's in between, this hot spot between the Metrodome and the University of Minnesota campus provides lots of choices for a great night out.

Uptown

This trendy area, centered near Lake Calhoun at Lake and Hennepin, has movie theaters featuring foreign and cult films, a variety of coffee shops and restaurants, several night spots, and wonderful bookstores and shops. Because of the eclectic nature of its surrounding establishments, the area's chief entertainment—especially during its annual art festival—is people watching.

The Milling District

This district's cobblestone roadway, old brick mills, beautiful park area, and bridge to Nicollet Island create a setting that recalls Minnesota's historic past. St. Anthony on the Main offers a fun setting to enjoy live music. On cold or rainy nights, romantics may want to wander into Nye's Polanaise Room, where locals gather around the piano bar for a musical escape to another time.

Bluff Creek Inn

guest once described the Bluff Creek Inn as a "romantic oasis in time." Indeed, the inn, set amid trees, fields, and flower beds less than a half-hour from the Twin Cities, has played refuge to many newlyweds as well as to harried two-career couples seeking a close and cozy respite. Time at the century-old house seems to stand still, and the property deed—signed by Abraham Lincoln—attests to the period reflected in its decor.

A veteran of the War of 1812 originally owned the property, but the house wasn't built until a German immigrant couple, the Vogels, purchased the property in 1854. The Vogels met and fell in love on their journey across the Atlantic, and somehow they ended up in Minnesota. They built their home on the Minnesota River bluffs using bricks from Minnesota River Valley clay. The house's dark hardwood floors—which gleam with polish and a century of footsteps—were milled from trees on the property. The inn's romantic history continues with its current proprietors, Anne and Gary Delaney, who met and married in

1988, soon after Anne acquired the old house.

Gary and Anne can entertain guests for hours with tales of romantic events at the inn. One couple visiting the inn liked it so much they decided to be married there on Valentine's Day. They invited a group of friends, but didn't tell them about their plans. With everyone sitting in the front parlor enjoying a glass of wine, the groom stood up and read his proposal, which he had published in that day's edition of the local newspaper. The minister, known only to the bride and groom, stood with his Bible and rendered the rest of the guests speechless. As soon as everyone stopped gasping and laughing, the couple was wed. Gary took charge of photographs while Anne led the crying.

The house was built using bricks of clay from the Minnesota River Valley. Its dark hardwood floors were milled from trees on the property.

Other couples have been married on the long front porch to the accompaniment of flutes and harps, and still others have used the large yard and gardens as the setting for their weddings. The Delaneys enjoyed each and every one. Many people who spent their wedding night at the inn return on their anniversary the following year.

Guests at Bluff Creek Inn are greeted in a small parlor decorated with flower-papered walls and a red oriental rug. Plaid wing chairs and love seat, arranged to invite conversation, surround a low tea table, and teddy bears line the steps to guest rooms on the second floor. The

Delaneys have furnished the house with antiques of a comfortable country design, and Anne likes to accessorize with the season. For instance, springtime visitors will find ceramic bunnies on the parlor's tiered table and topiary rabbits, Easter eggs, and rabbit napkin rings on the dining room table.

The inn boasts four guest rooms, each with its own private bath and two with fireplaces. Elizabeth's Room—papered and carpeted in a deep forest green—features a four-poster bed made of rich cherry and covered with a pretty pink flowered quilt that matches the curtains. A glass case table holding Wedgewood dishes and a decanter of sherry with two small crystal liqueur glasses rests beside the bed, and two pink wing chairs arranged near a small fabric-topped table complete the setting. A window-paned door opens onto a small deck where two chairs offer a lofty view of the property. An antique bride's gown and lace parasol hang on the wall, and old wedding photos in antique frames complete the tableau. A curtained doorway opens to the bathroom, where the theme is continued with dried flower arrangements and a miniature corset and bloomers on a tiny wooden hanger.

Saying "I love you"
NORWEGIAN
Jeg alska dag

Next to Elizabeth's is My Sister's Room, a smaller suite that feels like springtime throughout the year. Brick walls, a ceiling fan, and pink striped and flowered wallpaper surround the one-hundred-and-ten-year-old green metal-framed bed at the room's center. White wicker chairs, antique glass lamps, and shelves holding books, towels, and curios add to the room's cheerful feeling, and a sitting porch makes the small room seem larger than it is. One especially creative young man staying in this room arrived early with champagne, balloons, and flowers, arranging them on the bed in the shape of a heart around some lacy lingerie to surprise his companion.

Sliding glass doors in the Hollyhock Cottage, a retreat built above the small barn, provide a view of the surrounding woods and fields.

Down the hall near the stairway is May's Room. Decorated in shades of blue with red and white accents, the room has the feel of a Scandinavian country home. A large, Victorian-style white-and-brass bed fills one corner of the bright, airy room. Norwegian tole paintings, blue-and-white collector plates, books, and dried flower arrangements rest on a high wooden shelf running along two walls of the room. A rocking chair, a large wing chair, and a small table with two chairs offer guests ample opportunity to sit back and relax.

If Sister's Room is a never-ending springtime, the last room, Emma's, is Christmas every day of the year. Red and green colors predominate in plaids on the wing chair and in the floral stripe of the wallpaper. A hand-carved, four-poster Norwegian pine bed complete with a carved headboard featuring pine cones and needles awaits visitors, as does a whirlpool tub, nestled into a corner of the cozy room. Gnomes on the bed and bookshelves, an antique wooden sled, and a nutcracker standing at attention all help to create the holiday spirit in every season.

Though each room at the inn makes a wonderful setting for a weekend getaway, perhaps the best spot at Bluff Creek Inn is the Hollyhock Cottage, a suite built above the small barn. Separate from the rest of the house, the award-winning cottage provides a getaway retreat. After climbing stairs to a spacious wooden deck, guests enter the elevated cottage through sliding glass doors that provide a view of the surrounding woods and fields.

The pine wood planks of the cottage's walls and ceiling add a cozy warmth. One corner houses a beautiful black and green marble fireplace that begs for a fire on all but the hottest of days. Inviting overstuffed slipper chairs rest in front of the fireplace, and a king-size bed awaits couples in an alcove. Fabric printed with a delicate combination of white and pink stripes and tiny pastel flowers complements the white wicker table, always set with china and crystal awaiting the breakfast delivered in a basket each morning. The most popular feature of this suite is a double jacuzzi tub, set on a raised platform to provide a clear view of the fireplace.

Anne and Gary—both capable cooks—serve a breakfast that is a feast for both the stomach and the eyes. The morning meal might include cinnamon-spiked coffee, assorted freshly baked rolls or muffins, honey butter, fruits,

50 Ways to Lure your Lover

Light some candles, turn on romantic music, and exchange a soothing massage.

juice, and main courses such as eggs florentine or mouth-watering pecan-and-liqueur topped french toast.

Because of its proximity to the Twin Cities
and its popularity among honeymooners,
weekends at Bluff Creek Inn need to be
booked well in advance.

The inn is only ten minutes from the
University Landscape Arboretum, and even
closer to the Chanhassen Dinner Theater, but
don't be surprised if you find that you'd
just as soon stay close to the bluffs and
the inn that nestles below them.

1161 BLUFF CREEK DR. • CHANHASSEN

612-445-2735

BROOKLYN CENTER
PART OF THE EARLE BROWN HERITAGE CENTER
COUNTRY INN BED AND BREAKFAST

Inn on the Farm

s our world becomes increasingly urbanized and our rural roots slip further behind us, the farms our grandparents grew up on become more romantic in our minds and memories. We see those old farmsteads as tidy buildings, painted bright red and trimmed in pure white. They are the farms we knew in story books, and the thought of them brings feelings of well being and peace.

Very few of us can go back to the old family farm and even fewer would ever find the farm of our dreams, but the city of Brooklyn Center has preserved one such farm. There the buildings, displaying fresh coats of red and white paint, face a long green avenue, surrounded by pools of water and nestled in the shade of a big old oak, as ducks and geese swim in a pond or waddle through the green grass.

This is the Inn on the Farm, part of Brooklyn Center's Earle Brown Heritage Center. First known as Brooklyn Farm and then the Earle Brown Farm, the Heritage Center takes its name from the man who lived on the farm from 1906 to 1963. Earle Brown donated the property to the University of Minnesota in 1947 after his wife died, hoping the school would use it as an experimental farm, but after he died, the University sold it to a developer. For a decade, the farm languished and fell into disrepair while the city and suburbs crept up on all sides. Finally in 1985, Brooklyn Center purchased fourteen acres on which the original farmstead complex stands. After a public vote, the city began its renovation, turning the farm into the Earle Brown Heritage Center, a convention complex complete with a combination bed-and-breakfast and country inn.

The inn is actually four buildings connected by a glass-enclosed walkway. As you enter the house, you find yourself in a reception room with high ceilings, dark wooden beams, and paneled walls, decorated to look as it did when Earle Brown was elected sheriff in 1920. A plush maroon velveteen love seat faces the fireplace, and wing chairs flank it on either side. A moose head hangs over the doorway to the porch, and snowshoes and a wooden airplane propeller fill the walls. Photos of Brown's mother, Jean, and his grandfather, Captain John Martin, the farm's original owner, sit on the fireplace mantel below a Remington print of a cattle roundup. Two of the inn's guest rooms are also housed in the main house. The Foreman's House, the next building down the walkway from the central house, also has two guest rooms, one upstairs and one on the main floor. Both face out onto the small pond.

Two more guest rooms lie across the hall from the Foreman's House, both at ground level. Both rooms resemble a cozy north-woods cabin, with the ceilings and walls paneled in mocha-colored wooden planks. One has

The Inn on the Farm is so close to the Twin Cities that a couple can easily get away after work, or one can stop by early in the day to prepare a special surprise for a loved one.

been designed to be completely accessible for people with disabilities. The last building at the end of the hallway houses five guest rooms, two rooms just above ground level and three up a single flight of stairs. One of the upper rooms is a suite, with a large sitting room just off from the bedroom, and all of the rooms have been painted or wallpapered in gentle, neutral tones.

The city carefully preserved the general character of the buildings while updating them to the level of comfort and convenience we have become accustomed to. Most of the rooms have a rather masculine feel; you won't find any flowery chintzes or lacy bed covers. This theme is particularly appropriate considering Earle Brown remained a bachelor farmer until his forties. Decorated with sturdy antique furniture, the rooms look authentic. Still, the furnishings prove functional as well. Pine wardrobes dating from the mid-1800s hide televisions behind their doors, while English tea tables and spindle or pine pencil poster beds complete each room. The bathrooms vary in size, but each boasts a jacuzzi.

One of the nice things about the Inn on the Farm is that it is so close to the Twin Cities that a couple can easily get away after work, or one can set up a special surprise for a loved one. One forward-thinking man arrived one afternoon and set bouquets of roses and other flowers around the room and tied balloons onto the four-poster bed. He had told his wife to pack an overnight bag. After dinner they stopped at the inn, where she was sure there wouldn't be room. He insisted that they go in and ask, and they were taken on a tour of the available rooms. When they got to the one he'd decorated, she realized she had been fooled and was delightfully surprised.

Across the green from the inn, farm buildings have been renovated and reconstructed as a convention/meeting complex. A perfect spot for wedding receptions, the bride and groom's honeymoon suite sits only a short stroll across the green after the wedding festivities have ended. The inn serves breakfast between 7:30 and 8:30 A.M. in the enclosed porch off the main house's sitting room.

Take time during your stay to wander the grounds. As you sit by the small pool where a fountain sculpture of children under an umbrella bubbles with water, try to picture the days when the big Belgian horses Earle Brown raised grazed in the fields. Known to be a gracious host, Earle Brown enjoyed having people stop by the farm to admire his livestock and grounds. He would be happy to know that people are still coming to his farm and finding peace and relaxation.

6150 SUMMIT DRIVE NORTH • BROOKLYN CENTER

612-569-6330 • 612-569-6320 (FAX)

INN IS OPEN YEAR ROUND

RESTAURANT OPEN FRIDAY AND SATURDAY EVENINGS

BY RESERVATION ONLY

COUNTRY INN IN THE HEART OF THE MINNEAPOLIS
MEDITERRANEAN CUISINE ON A MISSISSIPPI RIVER ISLAND
MOST TABLES OVERLOOK THE RIVER

Nicollet Island Inn

Most couples seeking a romantic getaway leave the city to escape to a country inn. The Nicollet Island Inn, however, offers a bit of the country in the heart of the city. This historic limestone building has stood firmly on Nicollet Island since the 1890s, when it was built as a box factory. It became a sash and door company and later the home to other manufacturing firms until the mid-1900s, when the Salvation Army converted it to a men's lodge. It served this purpose until 1974, when the inn's developers purchased it.

For many years Nicollet Island had languished beneath weeds and misuse. In recent years, the island has reemerged as the beautiful green space in the middle of the Mississippi it once was. Today, joggers, bikers, walkers, skaters, and lovers dot the trails that crisscross the island. On the east side of the island, an antique iron bridge connects the island to the riverbank.

The entire Minneapolis downtown business district rises above the riverbank to the left of the inn, offering guests on its full-service patio, in the dining room, and in some guest rooms a chance to watch darkness fall as the nighttime glitter of city lights illuminates the river. On the patio, the soothing sound of the river's rushing water muffles the noise of the nearby city, and the thick stone walls of the inn hush the clamor of engines and sirens.

The second and third floors house all twenty-four of the inn's guest rooms, easily accessed by an elevator located directly across from the front desk. However, guests choosing to walk up the wide stairs will enjoy the Audubon prints of ducks and game birds, paintings of hunt scenes, and turn-of-the-century pastoral paintings that grace the walls.

Each guest room boasts high ceilings and walls—papered and decorated with a country estate theme—that surround either a four-poster or a brass bed. Louvered wooden shutters fit into the tall windows allow guests to dictate the amount of light in the room. The window's views range from city skyline to riverbank to tree-filled park and other historic buildings. Comfortably appointed with wing chairs and love seats, the rooms are perfect for reading or watching the televisions cleverly hidden inside tall armoires. If you want to jacuzzi, however, call ahead. Only two of the guest rooms have spas.

The Nicollet Island Inn offers two packages for couples

On the patio, the soothing sound of the river's rushing water muffles the noise of the nearby city, and the thick stone walls of the inn hush the urban clamor.

wishing a complete escape. The Getaway Package includes room accommodations, a bottle of premium champagne, a tray of assorted fruits and cheeses, breakfast for two in the hotel restaurant, and a morning newspaper to leisurely read in your room. The Island Package uses the Getaway plan as its base and adds a dinner for two in the inn's restaurant. While including many continental dishes, the inn's menu features a special "Minnesota Made" section, a sampling of indigenous Midwest foods prepared with a Mediterranean twist. This unique addition makes dining at the restaurant a regional treat, matching the management's focus on the area's roots prevalent throughout the inn.

Choose walleye and scallop cakes with Minnesota pesto or Minnesota goat cheese with wild rice croutons to start your Minnesotan meal. Smooth and creamy with a ripe but not overly strong flavor, the goat cheese is delicious when spread on the crunchy croutons baked right on the premises. Pureed and made into a mousse, sliced into patties and fried in olive oil, the mild tasting walleye and scallops are accompanied by a tangy corn pepper compote. The soup or salad course offers a choice of wild greens with apple cider vinaigrette or traditionally harvested wild rice bisque. The colorful salad includes a bouquet of wild edibles such as arugula and baby oak leaves, and the vinaigrette gives the greens a tangy sweetness. The smoky, peppery taste of the thick wild rice bisque with bits of bacon, is enhanced by red bell pepper cream sauce drizzled across the top, which adds even more color and taste.

Guests have three choices for their main dish. The first, Minnesota walleye, comes prepared as a filet, coated and cooked in crunchy sesame seeds with a chive-infused malt vinegar. To give the meal a "fish 'n' chips" theme, warm

Red River potato chips, waffle cut and lightly fried, accompany the walleye. Those in a nostalgic mood will enjoy Minnesota meat loaf with homemade catsup, served with sweet garlic mashed potatoes and mushroom gravy and a vegetable appropriate to the season—the kind of meal mom used to make, but with a bit more creativity and daring. The third choice, salt-and-pepper-cured pan-fried chicken with Lena's Hot Dish, acts as the inn's tribute to Minnesota's Scandinavian heritage and unique cuisine.

The inn's menu features a special "Minnesota Made" section, a sampling of indigenous Midwest foods prepared with a Mediterranean twist.

Plentiful servings remain true to Minnesota hospitality, so pace yourself to save room for one of the delicious desserts. The selections may change over seasons, but you can expect ice cream to play an important role in most and fresh, locally grown berries to enhance summer offerings. Espresso, cappuccino, cafe au lait, and Hallie's tea—which is a black tea mixed with flower petals and other fragrant herbs—as well as a fine selection of cognacs are available to accompany dessert.

The dining room offers an inviting space. Oak woodwork frames the large windows that look out on the Mississippi, glass-shaded candle lanterns glow softly on tables set with white linen, and bow-backed chairs surround black iron claw-foot tables. For couples, corner tables with padded benches allow lovers to snuggle close or hold hands.

Guests can wait for a table or enjoy an after-dinner drink in the small bar adjacent to the dining room. In this intimate sitting area with wing chairs, the bar's fireplace burns even in the summer.

You don't need to be a guest of the hotel to enjoy the restaurant's fine cuisine, as it is open to the general public. They also serve breakfast and lunch which includes a mini-version of the Minnesota Made evening menu.

Don't hesitate to ask the friendly staff at the Nicollet Island Inn for help planning a romantic interlude. One man employed several staff members to set up his engagement night. He wanted to capture the proposal on video, so he asked the manager to do the filming surreptitiously. They concealed the camera behind a lily, but as the couple waited for their dessert, the manager found he couldn't start the camera. Told to stall, the couple's waiter meticulously cleaned crumbs from their table and engaged in the longest small talk of his career. Finally, the manager called the potential groom to a fictitious phone call to find out how to start the camera. In the meantime, other diners began to sense something unusual in the air. When the ring finally arrived and the young Romeo went down on his knee, the woman at the next table and the bride-to-be both broke into tears, while the rest of the diners burst into applause. The camera caught it all.

95 MERRIAM ST. • MINNEAPOLIS

612-331-1800

EDINA
SOUTHWESTERN CUISINE
CASUAL ATTIRE WELCOME

Tejas

The Southwestern atmosphere of Tejas warms couples and relationships like the hot desert sun. If winter activities keep you in frigid Minnesota, an evening at Tejas will allow you, for a few hours, to imagine yourself soaking up the sun on a sandy southern beach. If you can't take your partner on a winter vacation, eat at Tejas and pretend.

Couples who enjoyed meeting in Tejas' downtown location will find a similar spirit in the new Edina restaurant—with a few enhancements. Alfresco dining is offered in the fountain-graced courtyard where summer seating is available at nine tables. Inside, stucco walls surround the eating area, which is open to the busy kitchen's bustling activity. The booths and wooden tables establish an informal atmosphere where casual attire is welcome. This could be the perfect place for couples to add a bit of fun to their evening by dressing in Western wear.

What did not change when Tejas moved to Edina is executive chef Mark Haugen's attention to detail. Haugen, the person responsible for the southwestern flavor of the food, attends as carefully to the appearance of each item on the menu as he does to its taste. He prefers an eclectic approach, preparing ingredients commonly thought of as Southwestern or Mexican with European cooking techniques and an emphasis on the French use of sauces. Staple ingredients include beans, corn, chiles, cilantro, garlic, and basil.

Two of the restaurant's fine soups exemplify the combination of great taste and beautiful presentation prevalent in Haugen's dishes. He arranges the black and white bean soup with epazote and red jalapeño cream in a yin/yang symbol, then scribbles red and green sauce across the top. With bits of avocado floating in the chicken-based broth, the tortilla soup offers a smokiness that comes not from the meat but instead from tomato, and a hint of cilantro emerges with each spoonful.

Diners preferring salad to soup should try the southwest caesar salad with cayenne croutons and cumin tamarind dressing. The snappy croutons and herbal dressing give this traditional salad flair and peppery zing.

Long and varied, the list of appetizers at Tejas includes smaller versions of many of the menu's entrees. These southwest specialties—quesadillas, tacos, nachos, enchiladas, and the like—may sound familiar, but Haugen's unique approach creates a wonderfully different dining experience. The chef adds smoked chicken, ginger-lime aioli, black bean puree, creamy barbecue sauce, and peanut-chipotle sauce to dishes, adding exciting taste as well as color. The taco shells are of blue corn tortillas, and the tomato salsa served with the smoked chicken nachos delivers a nice, slow warmth to the tip of the tongue. If you order the artichoke-pablano pizza, plan on sharing; its center, a fully-roasted garlic bulb, just might put a damper on a romantic evening out.

The menu also features a unique pan-fried pepper steak. Traditional ingredients—meat, potatoes, and vegetables—are all there, but they're prepared in a way you've never experienced. The steak, smothered in peppers, rests on a bed of fluffy white potatoes enhanced with the zip of horseradish. Corn, tomato aioli, and mustard greens give the plate a beautiful color and your palate more mouthwatering tastes.

The many exciting and delicious choices on the Tejas menu often cause couples to nibble off each others plates. The restaurant encourages this behavior on Valentine's Day by offering couples a four-course meal for two featuring samples of various dishes. Occasionally, the restaurant offers its "Taste of Tejas," a special presentation of ten to twelve different dishes.

If you have room left after your meal or simply stop by after a show, make sure to sample something from the dessert list, where the menu's French influence becomes most obvious in the decadent, calorie-soaked delights of the Southwest. The light and creamy coconut flan with strawberries and cajela (a caramel goat cheese sauce) rivals the best flan found north of the Rio Grande. The white chocolate–banana ice cream cake with roasted banana salsa and hot fudge takes the old-fashioned banana split into new territory: the bananas are pureed in the salsa and served warm on a bed of whipped cream. Other desserts come with Mexican vanilla sauce, whiskey butter sauce, fiery fudge sauce, and mandarin-caramel sauce, making it hard for diners to say no.

3910 WEST 50TH ST. • EDINA

612-926-0800

HOURS: MONDAY–THURSDAY, 11:00 A.M.–10:00 P.M.

FRIDAY, 11:00 A.M.–11:00 P.M.

SATURDAY, 10:00 A.M.–11:00 P.M.

SUNDAY, 10:00 A.M.–9:00 P.M.

OPEN SEVEN DAYS A WEEK

CLOSED NEW YEAR'S DAY, THANKSGIVING, CHRISTMAS DAY

MINNEAPOLIS WAREHOUSE DISTRICT
CARIBBEAN-STYLE RESTAURANT

Chez Bananas

ooking for a fun place for an ice-breaking first date? Or how about some great food when you and your honey are feeling too playful to put up with formality of a fine restaurant? Well, in a corner of the Textile Building in Minneapolis' lively Warehouse District lies Chez Bananas, an eatery where the atmosphere is as fun as the food is delicious. Here it's not only okay to play at the dinner table, it's encouraged.

Co-owner Joe Tachovski got his start in Madison, Wisconsin, with a very small Mexican take-out operation housed in an old shoe repair shop. Joe decorated the restaurant's two display windows with a bizarre beach tableau where GI Joe and Barbie dolls fought off plastic alligators. Inside, customers waiting in line were provided with windup toys for something to do. When Joe and co-owner Val Barnhart opened Chez Bananas in 1987, he brought the toys along. A Ouija board sits propped in a windowsill next to five Mr. Potato Heads, while plastic fish, lobsters, and crabs lie tangled in cotton netting draped across a window. Two plastic inflated snakes coil around the round support posts with tongues out in a perpetual hiss, and—just to remind you that you're still in Minnesota—giant inflated mosquitoes hang in suspended animation above.

> *White linen tops the tables, each of which holds a small nosegay of bright, fresh flowers—as well as a Magic 8 Ball and a mini Etch-A-Sketch.*

The interior of the restaurant boasts the typically high warehouse ceiling with exposed duct work and slowly rotating ceiling fans. The white brick walls contrast with the glossy black of window frames, support beams, radiators, and chairs. White linen tops the tables, each of which holds a small nosegay of bright, fresh flowers as well as a Magic 8 Ball and a mini Etch-A-Sketch. Both toys are tough to keep your hands off—offering an alternative to fiddling with the silverware for couples not yet completely at ease.

The Magic 8 Ball also comes in handy for diners who can't make up their mind which mouth-watering meals to choose. The Caribbean menu is an international delight, offering foods representing the many cultures that colonized the islands—including French, Spanish, East Indian, Asian, and British—as well as the indigenous Indian populations. In this eclectic combination of tastes you'll find curry, lime, peanuts, coconut, creole sauce, ginger, and garlic used in flavorful and fanciful ways with beef, chicken, pork, and shrimp.

Four lines of large, plastic multicolored letters spell out the daily specials, adding another playful touch to this dining funhouse. An assortment of appetizers—from wonderfully crisp black bean nachos with salsa to spicy creole chicken with tortillas—introduce diners to the Caribbean style. The main dishes, each served with rice, black beans, and freshly baked corn bread, sport names as colorful as their appearance. Try, for example, chiles rellenos in yaya sauce, ginger jerk chicken, or peanut barbecue pork medallions. A wide range of spiciness and heat accompanies the main dishes; though most are relatively tame, diners with a bold taste will want to try the Caribbean barbecue. The most popular item, coconut banana shrimp, mixes pieces of banana with creamy coconut milk to create a sweet sauce used to coat large pieces of shrimp—a rich, heavenly Caribbean treat.

Save room for dessert, because, along with coconut, the restaurant's namesake plays a major role in the tempting treats. Lime coconut cream pie and chocolate banana cheesecake, both made right on the premises, are just two of the menu's many Caribbean-inspired delights. The first, reminiscent of key lime pie, is light and airy with an added kiss of coconut, while the rich, smooth, and creamy cheesecake rests on top of a crunchy, sweet crust. A choice of four dessert wines—pear

50
Ways
to
Lure your Lover

Buy a blank jigsaw puzzle, write a love note on it, disassemble the puzzle, and give it to your lover.

or raspberry liqueur, port, and a very sweet Gewurtztraminer—offers a lush accompaniment to the banana treats. Five types of coffee, including two iced, also complement desserts.

If you still have doubts whether you and that special someone will enjoy a night out at Chez Bananas, just ask your own Magic 8 Ball. The answer will most likely read, "It is certain."

129 N. 4TH ST. • MINNEAPOLIS

612-340-0032

HOURS: SUNDAY, 5:00 P.M.–9:00 P.M.

MONDAY, 5:00 P.M.–10:00 P.M.

TUESDAY–THURSDAY, 11:30 A.M.–10:00 P.M.

FRIDAY, 11:30 A.M.–11:00 P.M.

SATURDAY, 5:00 P.M.–11:00 P.M.

EDINA
LOCATED IN RENOVATED CHURCH BUILT IN 1870S
MULTINATIONAL CUISINE

The Tour Cafe

he Tour Cafe may take its name from co-owner Greg LeMond's fame as the winner of the 1989 Tour de France, but credit the culinary skills of his partner, chef Scott Kee, for the Edina restaurant's growing reputation. Kee revamped the restaurant and its menu in 1993, and its popularity rocketed despite its evenings only hours.

The restaurant's four dining areas seat fifty-eight patrons. The two smaller rooms house only three tables, making an intimate space for quiet, romantic dining. Decorated in a soft shade of cream with dark teal carpeting and linenless tables, the rooms' only artwork consists of large, colorful Graham Watson photos of Tour de France race scenes. LeMond appears in some, and the famous yellow biking jersey he wore in the 1989 race greets visitors as they enter the building.

For a truly romantic dining experience at The Tour Cafe, make sure to visit in the summer when their cozy, multileveled patio is open. The terrace's large birch tree shades diners, and porous limestone rocks bubble with water, adding natural dinner music to the space. Ornamental vegetation shaped and pruned gives the patio the feeling of a large bonsai garden.

Visit in the summer when the multileveled patio is open. The terrace's large birch tree shades diners, and porous limestone rocks bubble with water.

The Tour Cafe's multinational cuisine has a spicy flair, a reflection of Kee's taste for food with a zip. While the menu offers a number of mild dishes for the tender of mouth, the best of Kee's cooking involves heat. The chef's signature Szechuan salmon with rice noodles and vegetable salad boasts thick and tender fish complemented by a coating of chopped pistachios and remnants of the chili oil it cooks in. The oil also lends its fire to the rice noodles and the colorful julienned vegetables served with the salmon, while rice wine vinegar and ginger add tang to the salad.

Kee's inspiration changes the menu regularly, but you can count on the Szechuan salmon and other favorites, such as an appetizer of curried shrimp egg rolls with roasted pineapple salsa, red pepper, and coconut juice.

Entrees of beef, pork, chicken, and a satisfying assortment of pastas grace the menu as well. Fresh-baked bread is presented before the main course, and—unless a sweet bread is served—guests are encouraged to dip the bread in the chili oil that sits on each table in a colored glass jar. The chili oil promises to warm you inside and out.

Wonderful desserts including homemade sherbets and

sorbets with fresh fruit complete your evening out at The Tour Cafe. The white pepper sangria sorbet served with the fruit salad surprises the taste buds as the initial cold, fruity blast slowly gives way to warmth spreading across the tongue and palate.

The restaurant offers a fine selection of wine, and stocks a variety of beers from microbreweries across the country. Most beers are available in double bottle size for couples who like to share.

4924 FRANCE AVE. SO. • EDINA

612-929-1010

HOURS: MONDAY–SATURDAY, 5:00 P.M.–10:00 P.M.

SUNDAY, 5:00 P.M.–9:00 P.M.

DOWNTOWN MINNEAPOLIS, NICOLLET MALL
COAT AND TIE RECOMMENDED

Goodfellow's

hile it's considered an American restaurant, don't expect to sit down in a T-shirt and jeans for burgers, fries, pizza, or pancakes at Goodfellow's. Its American fare focuses on familiar, regional recipes prepared in daring and creative ways, and, although not absolutely necessary, a coat and tie are recommended for men. The elegant Minneapolis restaurant takes its name from the original moniker of the Daytons department store across the street, once a dry goods store by the name of Goodfellow's—a tip of the hat to one of the co-owners, a Dayton family member.

Soothing salmon-colored walls accented with marble panels near the ceiling surround the restaurant's dining area. Small spotlights focused on the ceiling create a diffuse, warm glow throughout the room, and tables are set with salmon-colored cloths and napkins, a simple yet elegant white place setting, and three wine glasses for each guest. A vase holding a single blossom graces each table.

Classical music plays softly in the background in the

large and open room. With hardly any dividers separating the tables, special grid work on the ceiling helps absorb sound so that even when the room is full of diners, conversation remains subdued, allowing couples to converse in low tones. Many tables are set up for just two people, and a comfortable distance between tables gives romancing diners a sense of privacy. With three servers assigned to each table—one to take your order and offer advice on wine selection, another to bring the food, and a third to clear—the attentive service staff adds another level of elegance to your dining experience.

It's the menu, however, that really sets Goodfellow's apart from other Minnesota eateries. Consider, for instance, the horseradish mashed potatoes, or the grilled salmon garnished with a colorful salsa on either side, or even the pork medallions, served with wild rice properly crunchy and nutty and accompanied by a vegetable stir-fry of crisp carrots, cabbage, zucchini, tomatoes, and green pea pods. The bread tray offers an eclectic assortment of breads and muffins all baked on site, and salads are crisp and as visually pleasing as they are tasty.

While many would consider the fare nouveau cuisine, some important differences distinguish Goodfellow's food from others. First, all entrees are served in generous

50
Ways
to
Lure your Lover

Treat each other to a limousine ride, dressing elegantly for the occasion.

> *The signature dessert is a lace cookie cup filled with whipped cream, with raspberries floating in a layer of swirled caramel sauce and white cream.*

portions so, though they remain true to the color and artistic arrangement of nouveau, one doesn't see more blank white plate than food. And while the food may be prepared in surprising new ways, it is still recognizable—no wildly exotic vegetables with unpronounceable names—and herbs and spices are used sparingly, so as not to dominate the food.

Couples should allocate at least two hours for a dining experience at Goodfellow's in order to dine slowly, leaving room for their fantastic desserts. The signature dessert is a lace cookie cup filled with whipped cream, with raspberries floating in a layer of swirled caramel sauce and white cream. Chocolate lovers will enjoy their fudge strudel with raspberries. Eighteen dessert wines, liqueurs, and excellent coffees are available to accompany your dessert. Goodfellow's also carries 18 choices of beer and an impressive 470 wine labels.

THE CONSERVATORY ON NICOLLET

800 NICOLLET MALL • MINNEAPOLIS

612-332-4800

HOURS: MONDAY–FRIDAY, 11:30 A.M.–2:00 P.M.

MONDAY–THURSDAY, 5:30 P.M.–9:00 P.M.

FRIDAY–SATURDAY, 5:30 P.M.–10:00 P.M.

CLOSED SUNDAYS AND HOLIDAYS

MINNEAPOLIS WAREHOUSE DISTRICT
NATURAL FOODS RESTAURANT
GOURMET NATURAL FOODS AND FRESH SEAFOOD

Cafe Brenda

wner Brenda Langton began working at her cafe, then the Cafe Kardamena in St. Paul, at the age of fifteen, waiting tables and working in the kitchen, learning the business from the ground up. Before she turned twenty-one, Brenda purchased the restaurant and changed its name. The restaurant, then little more than a hole in the wall, offered an intimate atmosphere, and the employees knew most of the customers on a first-name basis. Vegetarian cooking had just started to find an audience, leaving the staff free to experiment with ideas and ingredients.

The versatile menu made the little restaurant a success, and in 1986 Brenda made a leap of faith and miles, crossing the river to open a bigger restaurant in the newly remodeled and resurging Warehouse District of downtown Minneapolis. With very high ceilings and walls almost completely filled with windows, Cafe Brenda has a bright and open feeling during the daylight hours. At night they turn the lights down low, and the intimacy of the original restaurant returns. On special holidays, small votive candles placed in the windows flicker soft yellow light, creating a romantic aura both within and without.

Billed as a Natural Restaurant Extraordinaire, Cafe Brenda serves fresh seafood and foods free of artificial ingredients and preservatives. Brenda visits the nearby Farmers' Market early in the morning, buying the freshest Minnesota-grown produce for the menu. Each day a few select specials are on the menu, as well as a regular appetizer, entree, and sandwich selection, desserts, and beverages.

Brenda visits the nearby Farmers' Market early in the morning, buying the freshest Minnesota-grown produce for the menu.

Guests at Cafe Brenda leave satisfied but never too full, confident they've eaten fewer chemicals, fats, and cholesterol than at most other restaurants. Whenever possible, Cafe Brenda serves organically grown food, including the bananas and coffee and the ingredients used to prepare the cornbread and sourdough.

Those who have not eaten at a natural foods restaurant have nothing to fear and much to anticipate. The soups include roasted onion and a delicious chick-pea pumpkin, a colorful, sweet combination of garbanzo beans and roasted pumpkin seeds, which add crunch and flavor. While rice, grains, and pastas predominate in the menu, a wide variety of fish, served baked, broiled, and in soups, is always available. A balance of herbs, spices, and vinegars adds zest and delicate aromas and flavors. The restaurant also offers a good selection of coffee, tea, soda, juice, beer, and wine.

A portion of the restaurant can be sectioned off for large groups, making Cafe Brenda a wonderfully different choice for wedding parties and rehearsal dinners. Also ideal for an intimate dinner for two, the cafe's small tables make conversation easy, as even whispers carry across to your dining companion. Spaced a comfortable distance apart from one another, the most sought-after tables sit near the windows. Reservations are suggested for weekends.

300 1ST AVE. N. • MINNEAPOLIS

612-342-9230

HOURS: MONDAY–FRIDAY, 11:30 A.M.–2:00 P.M.

MONDAY–THURSDAY, 5:30 P.M.–9:30 P.M.

FRIDAY AND SATURDAY, 5:30 P.M.–10:00 P.M.

CLOSED SUNDAYS

DOWNTOWN MINNEAPOLIS
SIXTY YEARS OF MEMORABLE OCCASIONS

Murray's Restaurant

urray's may not be an intimate club— it's not really a place for couples to get together privately and hold hands in secluded and dark corners—but it does offer a different kind of romance. Decorated with curtains and mirrors, filled with guests in evening dress, voices drifting over tables set very near to one another, the restaurant creates a setting straight out of a Bogie and Bacall film, celebrating the style and grace of the 1940s.

The last of the family-run, single name restaurants like Charlie's, Sheik's, and Harry's, Murray's has served generations of loyal guests, a following created through fond memories of special evenings of great service and delicious food. First opened in 1933 as Murray's Red Feather, the restaurant moved to its present location in 1946, dropped "Red Feather" along the way, and soon became the place for those who wanted to see and be seen. Since that time, Murray's has played host to famous athletes, politicians, media people, and other local celebrities. Its highly trained staff, which has seen very little turnover through the years, provides friendly service to the many repeat guests.

Murray's is the last of a breed, and proud of it. Instead of completely changing the restaurant's look during remodelling in the 1980s, Patrick Murray, son of the original owners, simply replaced the old and worn furnishings with new materials in the same colors. The old piano bar that once filled a good portion of the front of the restaurant has been reduced in size to expand the dining room and kitchen. A complete success, Murray's renovation allows more room for both diners and kitchen staff while maintaining the traditions of the restaurant, and people who have patronized Murray's for forty years feel just as comfortable and at home as they did in the original setting.

The dining room's atmosphere helps cast diners back in time. The melodic strains of violins and piano fill the background. The walls, covered in a rose moiré satin, match the pink draperies and valances that divide the room into sections. Electric chandeliers mounted on the walls and ceiling cast a warm glow reflected in mirrored pillars.

50 Ways
to
Lure your Lover

Put on your best

Bogart and Bacall

costumes and

share a lunch

straight out of

the movies.

The dinner menu includes a wide selection of chops and prime rib, as well as the lighter fare of chicken and

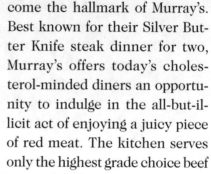

Take a full day to enjoy downtown Minneapolis and then stop at Murray's for high tea, a perfectly civilized break.

fish. Steaks, however, have become the hallmark of Murray's. Best known for their Silver Butter Knife steak dinner for two, Murray's offers today's cholesterol-minded diners an opportunity to indulge in the all-but-illicit act of enjoying a juicy piece of red meat. The kitchen serves only the highest grade choice beef raised in the corn belt. Dry-aged and processed the old-fashioned way, the steaks are selected by Murray's own meat cutter, who inspects the five tons of beef the restaurant serves each month for correct marbling, size, and aging.

Murray's has recently embarked on an impressive development of their wine cellar for those diners who enjoy wine with their dinner. They currently list over four hundred wines and constantly evaluate those in stock and those coming on the market, updating the wine list every six weeks. The service staff—highly knowledgeable about the wines—will happily help you select one to complement your entree.

The restaurant also boasts its own on-site bakery where they daily prepare breads and desserts. Some of the special breads include garlic toast, pretzel rolls, and black bread. For dessert, enjoy the angel pie with lemon meringue crust or the marvelous pecan pie. A mocha java royale complements any dessert and completes the Murray's dining experience.

If you and your partner are willing to have an early meal, between 4 and 6 P.M., Murray's offers the Downtowner Menu, which includes many of the entrees from the standard dinner menu at a reduced price. Dining off the Downtowner makes it easier on the pocketbook for couples planning an evening at the theatre or a concert after dinner.

Another special service offered at Murray's is their high tea, served between 2 and 4:30 P.M. Take a full day to enjoy the new and exciting developments in downtown Minneapolis and then stop at Murray's for a perfectly civilized break. The menu appropriately includes fresh-baked scones with clotted cream, tea cakes and pastries, and finger sandwiches. A wide selection of teas is available, as are dry sherry and ruby port wine. Stepping outside after tea time, you almost expect to hear Big Ben chime and see a red double-decker bus roll by.

Over the years, staff members at the restaurant have seen a fair share of marriage proposals. One woman proposed to a man by putting a ring in the bottom of his champagne glass; other rings have been placed in bread baskets and under napkins. Men have also gotten down on their knees, which is quite a challenge with the tables so close together. Of course, many couples return on their anniversaries, often requesting the same table where they enjoyed their first date years before.

26 SOUTH SIXTH ST. • MINNEAPOLIS

612-339-0909

HOURS: MONDAY–FRIDAY, 11:00 A.M.–3:00 P.M.

MONDAY–FRIDAY, 2:00 P.M.–3:30 P.M. FOR HIGH TEA

MONDAY–THURSDAY, 4:00 P.M.–10:30 P.M.

FRIDAY–SATURDAY, 4:00 P.M.–11:00 P.M.

SUNDAY, 4:00 P.M.–10:00 P.M.

CLOSED ON ALL MAJOR HOLIDAYS

NEAR CONVENTION CENTER AND ORCHESTRA HALL
SPICY CHINESE CUISINE

Ping's Szechuan Bar & Grill

In 1975, nine years after he arrived in the United States from his native Vietnam, chef Minh Quuoc Tran opened Ping's Szechuan Bar & Grill, a popular and successful restaurant that stands as a tribute to the owner's drive and creativity.

Located just a block from the Convention Center and a short distance from Orchestra Hall, Ping's offers a dining experience unlike any other Asian restaurant. Even the decor is different, missing the gold dragons and the red or green color scheme often found in such establishments. Instead, the sleek and sophisticated two-tiered dining space centers on its full-length windows, allowing in lots of light and providing a view of the busy sidewalks outside.

The traditionally colorful, spicy, and hot Szechuan cuisine comes from China's western mountain region. Some favorites from Ping's menu include volcano scallops (large scallops stir fried in spicy kung po sauce, nestled in a bed of sliced carrots and surrounded by steamed broccoli), Ping's wings (chicken wings stir-fried in a hot sauce with sweet

red pepper and scallions), and pot stickers (Chinese dumplings stuffed with seasoned pork and served steamed or
fried). Spicy kung po sauce is used on many dishes, as are
hoisin, red peppers, and onions.
Tiny "boxes" help diners iden-
tify the spicier items on the
menu, but if you're not sure how
much heat you can handle, ask
your server for suggestions.

Order several spicy

items and share.

"Happiness shared is

happiness multiplied."

Diners seeking more famil-
iar dishes will find fried rice, egg
foo young, chop suey, chow
mein, and lo mein on the menu.
With so many wonderful options, couples should order dif-
ferent items and share, in keeping with Ping's philosophy
that "happiness shared is happiness multiplied."

The wine list has a helpful explanation of how to
choose wines to complement Asian cuisine, and Ping's
considerately offers all wines by the glass as well as the
bottle. The dessert list offers a nice assortment of cheesecakes and tarts, but after a spicy meal, diners may wish to
cool their palates with a sorbet or ice cream. The house
specialty is litchi nut sorbet.

1401 NICOLLET AVENUE • MINNEAPOLIS

612-874-9404

HOURS: MONDAY–FRIDAY, 11:30 A.M.–2:00 P.M. BUFFET LUNCH

MONDAY–THURSDAY, 11:00 A.M.–10:00 P.M.

FRIDAY, 11:00 A.M.–MIDNIGHT

SATURDAY, NOON–MIDNIGHT

SUNDAY, NOON TO 9:00 P.M.; 5:00 P.M.–9:00 P.M. DINNER BUFFET

$\mathcal{A}$dditional $\mathcal{R}$estaurants

Couples out for dinner in the Minneapolis
area might also try one of these
fine establishments.

Christos Greek Restaurant

2632 NICOLLET AVE. SO. • MINNEAPOLIS

612-871-2111

A bright and airy place for lunch, this authentic Greek restaurant offers nothing on their menu that hasn't passed the test of the owner's mother, who scrutinizes each item's authenticity. Greek landscapes and seascapes spread across white walls while Greek music plays in the background; for a moment you can almost imagine yourself on the Greek Isles, the deep blue Aegean sea just outside. Diners should come prepared for some unusual spice combinations. Cinnamon, for example, adds a unique touch to the rice pilaf. The menu includes excellent kabobs, vegetarian moussaka, and Koupepia-Cyprus dolmades. A sampler plate is available for the indecisive, and most diners will want to start their meals with a hummus, tahini, or tsitsiki appetizer.

The Malt Shop

50TH AND BRYANT AVE. SO. • MINNEAPOLIS

612-824-1352

Lots of wood, plenty of booths, big burgers, and even bigger malts take diners at the Malt Shop back to the days when rock and roll was young, yet it refreshingly lacks the signs and photos that adorn most fifties-style eateries. They serve not only delicious, unpretentious burgers but a diverse menu of options, including hot and cold vegetarian sandwiches and salads. The restaurant fulfills the promise of its name with thick malts in frosty metal shakers large enough for couples to enjoy one with two straws. Performers occasionally add piano, acoustic guitar, and soft voices to the air. The high booth walls allow for intimate conversations.

Pracna on Main

117 SE MAIN ST. • MINNEAPOLIS

612-379-3200

This historic dining saloon on the Minneapolis riverfront serves good food, but many diners remember it most for the bowl of Legos on each table. Outdoor tables provide curbside service along a brick roadway, and twenty tap beers await even the most discriminating taste buds. This establishment originally opened in 1890, closed for prohibition, reopened in what was then a very seedy neighborhood, closed, and finally reopened during a recent riverfront revival. It deserves to be discovered again.

Figlio

3001 HENNEPIN AVE. • MINNEAPOLIS

612-822-1688

This popular bistro is located in the South Minneapolis Uptown area at Lake and Hennepin. You can enjoy people watching, wonderful wood-oven-baked pizzas to accompany your drinks, and a full menu for a complete night out.

Shelley's Woodroast

6501 WAYZATA BOULEVARD • ST. LOUIS PARK

612-593-5050

Like the Inn on the Farm, this establishment takes you out and into the country. The log structure and decor speak of the north woods. They offer terrific wood-roasted food and a nice selection of local beers, which you can sample by ordering a taster. Have a plate of walleye fingers to accompany your beer tasting.

Walker Art Center & Loring Park

With the world-renowned Guthrie Theatre and the Walker Art Institute, which includes a wonderfully eclectic sculpture garden, the Walker Art Center offers couples an opportunity to make an afternoon or evening out a cultural experience. See the latest exhibit or newest play and walk among the sculpture before crossing the unique bridge, which is itself a piece of art, to Loring Park and its starburst fountain, pathways, and nearby lineup of cafes at which to end the evening with a nightcap.

Minnesota

The Woods & Prairie

The vast expanse of prairie and forest that extends across much of Minnesota offers a multitude of sites for a romantic getaway. Some are hidden deep in the woods, others grace the main streets of historic towns.

On your journey across the state, make time to stop at one of the state parks that are located within easy distance of almost all retreats. While all of Minnesota's state parks make beautiful places for couples to escape to, consider one of the less visited areas described here if you are looking for privacy.

Itasca
The source of the Mississippi River makes a symbolic site for new beginnings. Enjoy your honeymoon outdoors.

Banning State Park
With magnificent river scenery including Wolf Creek Falls, this relatively uncrowded park offers privacy along with its beautiful views.

Beaver Creek Valley
Perfect for hot days, you'll relax next to a cool, spring-fed stream in the shade of a hardwood forest.

Maplewood
Rolling landscape, a variety of lakes, and relative privacy make this a great place for couples to find their own special corner. Its nine thousand acres are the least visited in the park system.

Romancing

Walden Woods Bed and Breakfast

Henry David Thoreau spent his time in Walden Woods in a very simple cabin he built for less than twenty-nine dollars next to the pond he made famous. When Anne and Dick Manly opened their log cabin bed-and-breakfast on Lake Mud, they knew naming it after the nearby lake could pose some marketing problems. Instead, they named their inn in honor of Thoreau's setting for his classic work.

Just as at Thoreau's Walden, wildlife abounds in this woodland setting. A pair of loons lives within view of the house since Dick built a nesting platform for them, and a heron rookery sits at the north end of the lake. An osprey has moved in with the herons, and as many as eight hummingbirds come to the feeders that hang in front of the cabin's screened porch, so guests can watch their buzzing antics within arm's length.

The logs on the outside of the cabin have weathered gray, but inside they glow with golden warmth. Two levels make up the guest portion of the house, including a dining area and sitting room whose large bay window offers a marvelous view of the lake. Shelves hold books and some of Dick's hand-carved wooden wild-life. French doors covered with lace panels lead to each of the main floor's two bedrooms. The Lakeview Room offers a great view of the lake, while the Jenny Lind Room across the hall takes its name from its high-styled Victorian bed. The room's decor follows the Victorian theme, including books of Victorian art and stories. A shared bath located between the two guest rooms features a claw-foot tub with a shower and a frosted pane of glass in the door.

50 Ways

to

Lure your Lover

Find a stable that offers sleigh rides during the winter months and bundle up for a nighttime ride.

Split log stairs lead to the upper level. Its sitting room features an antique chair, a forerunner of today's recliner, with leather padding, ornately carved wooden armrests, and a leg rest tucked under the seat that pulls forward as the back of the chair reclines. Grandma's Attic, one of the guest rooms, boasts a brass bed and antique ladies' clothing hanging on the wall. A telescope allows guests to pick out the tiniest bird in the forest or the distant valleys on a full moon. With twin beds, the Trapper's Room may not be the first choice for couples on a romantic getaway. It looks as though Davy Crockett just checked out: snowshoes and steel traps hang on the log walls next to a beaver, coyote, and raccoon pelts, while Hudson Bay blankets cover the beds. The bathroom on this floor is small, with just enough room for a shower, sink, and commode.

The hosts serve an appropriately hearty breakfast of juice, fresh fruit, freshly-baked muffins or fruit bread, waffles or pancakes served with real maple syrup, eggs, and sausages. Nothing beats a relaxing walk after a filling breakfast, and Walden Woods makes a great escape for couples who enjoy the outdoors. Dick has cut and groomed hiking and cross-country ski trails on the property and provides guests with a small map

Walden Woods makes a great escape for couples who enjoy the outdoors.

of the trail system. Nearby Kathio State Park has even more cross-country ski trails, and numerous antique shops in the area offer a chance for leisurely browsing. The cabin also makes a great place to simply curl up on a sofa, listen to the breeze blow through the trees, and sink into the pages of a good novel.

The history of the cabin abounds in romance. Anne and Dick met while he was building the house and their love grew as the home did. They count Jim Lang among the many who have enjoyed relaxing in peace and quiet at the cabin with a loved one. Jim, of course, is the longtime host of *The Dating Game.*

16070 HIGHWAY 18 SE • DEERWOOD

612-692-4060 FOR RESERVATIONS

CALLAWAY (NORTH OF DETROIT LAKES)
300-ACRE RESORT: ROOMS, CABINS, LODGE, SAUNAS
HOME OF THE BOTTOMLESS COOKIE JAR

Maplelag

In late autumn, when most of Minnesota's resorts begin to close for the season, Maplelag gears up for its busiest time of the year. In the fall, special events like mountain biking and Scottish flings, along with the wondrous colors of the surrounding maple and hardwood forest, keep guests flowing in. As winter snows cover the resort's surrounding three hundred acres, visitors come to enjoy the fifty-three kilometers of groomed cross-country ski trails.

The resort rests on land traditionally used by the Ojibwa as a source of sugar. They tapped many of its trees each spring, as owners Jim and Mary Richards did for fourteen years. In fact, Maplelag actually began as a maple sugar operation before Jim and Mary opened it as a resort. It's located just north of Detroit Lakes in the northwestern region of the state, a one-hour drive from Fargo-Moorhead, four and a half hours from the Twin Cities, and four hours from Winnipeg.

The main lodge and many of the cabins have been

built of wood taken from the surrounding forest, so their interior walls and beams form a pleasing mix of light and dark wood with a variety of grains and textures. An abundance of light-colored aspen and basswood, combined with the lodge's big open spaces, creates an airy, bright space. Light playing through the almost sixty stained glass windows set at different levels and angles and scattered throughout the building adds color and an enchanted feeling to the lodge. Maplelag also offers meeting/reading rooms, including a large room on the second level divided into cozy nooks with booths, benches, and tables for game playing, conversation, or just quiet reading.

Framed memorabilia dating back through the beginning years of the resort and beyond covers the walls; a glass case contains early maple syruping equipment used by the Ojibwa and early settlers. Jim also collects antique fish decoys and plans to open a small museum on the premises to house them. The resort also has an alcove built with ascending steps that serves as seating for Saturday nights, when guests often join together to present a free-wheeling, improvisational talent show.

> *Light playing through the almost sixty stained glass windows set at different levels and angles and scattered throughout the building adds color and an enchanted feeling to the lodge.*

Maplelag serves three meals a day on oak or pine picnic-style tables in its large dining room. For breakfast, the kitchen offers its own special blend of hot cereal, pancakes, eggs, and a side order of meat.

Lunches usually include a hearty soup and sandwich combination. Guests visiting on a Sunday won't want to miss the Scandinavian smorgasbord: two tables spread with cold cuts, boiled eggs, kippers, pickled herring, muffins, breads, sausages, oysters, fruit soup, and cheeses, including traditional jarlsberg, gjetost, sugblue, and Danish havarti.

> *The small cabins make a cozy retreat for couples who have spent the day exploring the open spaces and enjoying the camaraderie found in the lodge.*

Between meals, guests can stop by the snack bar near the kitchen on the first floor, where hungry skiers can find coffee, tea, and hot cider, along with four large jars continually filled with fresh-baked cookies.

The main lodge also houses two guest rooms, but the majority of guests stay in the scattered cabins or in two new buildings—the Northern Pacific and the Great Northern. The Great Northern has thirteen bedroom units designed for couples. Three of the cabins—Sauva Sauna, the Sod Roof Cabin, and the Coop—accommodate just couples, and the Sauva Sauna has a wood stove. The small cabins make a cozy retreat for couples who have spent the day exploring the unrestricted open spaces and enjoying the camaraderie found in the lodge.

In between skiing, relaxing in the lodge, and eating delicious and plentiful meals, guests can also enjoy the sauna, steam room, twenty-three-foot hot tub, or even a professional massage. The lodge boasts two saunas—one

for suits and one "sans suits"—including a traditional Finnish "smoke" sauna, fired by wood that fills the air with a
pleasant, smoky scent. For those determined to sample
the complete ritual of Finnish saunas, Jim will cut a hole
in the lake ice and the brave (or foolish) can plunge in
after emerging from the heat.

Reservations at Maplelag are made on the American
plan, which combines meals and rooms in one charge for
added convenience. Weekends in the winter months can
be booked a year in advance. For the most romantic, quiet
occasions, come early or midweek.

*Take a late night full moon ski, with the
temperatures low enough to make you keep
up a good pace, then return to the main lodge
and submerge your bodies in the steaming
hot tub under glittering stars or share a
sauna. Either way you emerge completely
relaxed and renewed.*

*Bring your own wine—they do not serve
alcohol at the resort, but you are welcome
to bring your own into the dining room or
lodge. Also you must provide your own
bedding and towels. While most people just
bring sleeping bags, why not make it really
special and bring some brand new sheets
along (satin maybe), a fluffy comforter, lots
of pillows, or maybe even a fake fur throw,
and pretend you're in the far reaches
of the Northwest Territories.*

RT. 1 • CALLAWAY

218-375-4466 • 800-654-7711

HISTORIC HOTEL IN PIPESTONE

The Days Inn Historic Calumet

Most visitors to Pipestone come to see Pipestone National Monument, a true gem of the prairie protecting a quartzite rock exposure that represents an ancient Precambrian shoreline and a centuries-old quarry where Native Americans gathered the soft red rock used for carving pipes. Couples visiting the historic town will want to spend the night—or weekend—at The Days Inn Historic Calumet, a wonderful old hotel constructed with local quartzites and pipestones whose distinct reddish color complements the nineteenth-century design.

The inn first opened in 1888, when two hundred people a day arrived in Pipestone on passenger trains, stopping on their way to settle the prairie and expand the country westward. Since the passenger trains are gone and the country has long since reached the shores of the Pacific, the hotel—one of twenty buildings in the community on the National Register of Historic Places—now caters to tourists, historians, and romantics. Its thirty-eight rooms have been uniquely restored, offering a relaxing retreat in two distinct styles—a 1950s motif and the inn's historical Victorian style using antiques from mansions in Louisiana, Boston, and England. While the older-styled rooms offer a more romantic feel (their names include "Hearts and Flowers," "I Promised You a Rose Garden," and "Anniversary Waltz"), both styles make staying at the inn a lot of fun.

The inn also incorporates a restaurant, lounge, pub, and gift shop. One interior wall is made entirely of Sioux quartzite. The dining room—with country-style artwork, colonial wallpaper, an embossed tin ceiling, and a magnificent quartzite fireplace—best exemplifies the eclectic atmosphere of the inn's decor. Couples will want to dine at one of the several tables recessed into cozy nooks. Antique plates hold dinners from a traditional American menu featuring beef and a wonderful salad bar.

Like many inns, the Calumet plays host to many weddings and honeymoons, a Christmas Festival of Trees, and a New Year's celebration. They also offer packages for couples, such as the "Pleasureful Affair," which includes a stay in one of the Victorian rooms, dinner for two, champagne, and a book of love poems. Couples may also wish to try the "Theater

50 Ways to Lure your Lover

Attend the song of Hiawatha Pageant in Pipestone in late July-early August. Read aloud Longfellow's poetic account of the famous romance.

Affair," where the inn combines a room, dinner for two, and an evening performance at the Pipestone Center for the Performing Arts.

MAIN AND HIAWATHA • PIPESTONE

507-825-5871 • 800-535-7610

TURTLE RIVER LAKE NEAR BEMIDJI
RECREATIONAL LOG CABIN RESORT

A Place In The Woods

f you and your mate want to find a cozy cabin for a romantic getaway, look no further than A Place In The Woods opened in 1991. Located on Turtle River Lake, the small resort offers many recreational opportunities, including boating, fishing, swimming, biking, horseshoes, and hiking; but, with the fine amenities, couples may want to spend much of their time indoors.

Each of the resort's ten cabins of lacquered white and red pine logs has a porch facing the water for enjoying warm summer days and a wood-burning stove next to a comfortable couch for snuggling up on cold winter nights. Hearts hang on the doors and embellish the dishes, fresh candles wait to light a romantic mood, and a small bouquet of wildflowers on the table greets guests arriving in summer. At other times of year, seasonal accents decorate the room. The cabins also include convenient and modern kitchenettes fully stocked with cooking utensils, dishes, and flatware, so couples unwilling to leave their cozy confines can cook for themselves.

While each cabin makes a wonderful retreat, the resort offers two special honeymoon cottages. The Kestrel lies near the lake, next to the Eagle's Nest Lodge, the resort's central building. Open spaces, such as the bedroom loft and the huge bathroom with an extra-large jacuzzi, create an airy feel to the cabin. The Whip-Poor-Will, the furthest cabin from the lake, offers a greater sense of privacy. A set of lace-curtained French doors separates the bedroom from the living room and kitchen area, creating a captivating effect. The glass displays the queen-size bed, covered in a floral spread and piled with plump pillows. A tray holding two wine glasses filled with chocolate kisses, with a silk rose resting in the center adds to the welcome. Guests who let the owners know they intend to celebrate a special romantic occasion during their stay will find champagne and balloons. The hosts thoughtfully provide thick towels and bubbling bath tablets for use with the bathroom's large, rose-colored jacuzzi .

Enjoy the solitude and peacefulness of your little cabin in the woods.

The lake and surrounding forty-five acres are worth exploring, so if you can force yourself away from the comfortable surroundings, hike on their self-guiding nature trail. A well-written booklet and the friendly resort retriever, Molly, will help you to find your way. To explore the lake, you can rent one of the resort canoes and paddle up to Moose Creek, where an abundance of wildlife lives along the shores. If you're quiet and lucky, you might encounter deer, porcupine, bear, eagles, loons, or, on the rarest occasion, a timber wolf.

If you somehow can't find enough to do at the resort, an eighteen-hole golf course is located near the resort, and the nearby Chippewa National Forest and Buena Vista Ski Area both offer plenty of cross-country ski trails. If you don't want to cook, you can drive the short distance into Bemidji to have dinner in one of several restaurants. Ask at the Eagle Nest Lodge for suggestions on where to eat. Most importantly, enjoy the solitude and peacefulness of your little cabin in the woods.

50
Ways
to
Lure your Lover

Go sailing,

canoeing, or

kayaking, or

charter a boat for

a carefree,

romantic sail.

11380 TURTLE RIVER LAKE ROAD N.E. • BEMIDJI

218-586-2345 • 800-676-4547

LAKE DARLING NEAR ALEXANDRIA
RECREATIONAL RESORT
GOLF, SWIMMING, FISHING, TENNIS, ARCHERY

Arrowwood—A Radisson Resort

How could you not find romance at a resort located on Lake Darling? Named for a straight shafted shrub that grows in the natural areas that are part of the resort's magnificent landscape, Arrowwood offers fun-loving couples a chance to stay by themselves in quiet seclusion or participate in a wide selection of recreational options.

The resort's buildings, decorated with soft pastel colors, wood details, and a country atmosphere, create a feeling of the country homes depicted in the paintings of Swedish artist Carl Larsson. In the Lake Cafe's dining room, for instance, guests find wainscoting and beams painted in shades of mint and rose, soft flowered carpet underfoot, and big leather armchairs. Tole paintings border the walls, and floor-to-ceiling windows look out onto the deep blue lake and the outdoor pool one level below. Narrow shelves holding collector plates line the walls, and whimsical hand-carved wooden sculptures depicting the daily tasks of a traditional Scandinavian homemaker sit atop newel posts scattered through-out the room.

The hallways and guest rooms at the resort also display more Carl Larsson paintings. Guests who call ahead for a room with a view of the lake will enjoy private balconies to sun-bathe, read, or simply relax in privacy. The rooms have TVs and VCRs, and the front desk offers a large selection of vid-eotapes for guest use. A new wing added to the resort in 1993 features suites with jacuzzis and fireplaces.

While the room service is impec-cable, guests may not want to stay in their rooms for long. At Arrowwood, you can get almost everything but bored. The management not only pro-vides numerous recreational opportu-nities for guests to participate in but also offers scheduled events on Friday, Saturday, and Sunday. Start the day with a fun run around Arrowwood's trails or an early round on the resort's eighteen-hole ex-ecutive golf course. Indoor and outdoor pools offer guests a place to swim no matter the weather, and shuffleboard tournaments, volleyball games, the "Rad-a-thon" (a series of fun and not-too-serious competitive events), wind-surf-ing clinics, and horseshoe tournaments guarantee guests plenty to do throughout the afternoon. The resort even puts on a fishing clinic Saturday mornings for guests who want to know where the fish are biting, and the marina

50
Ways
to
Lure your Lover

The right music can add instant romance. Outdoors, bring along a cordless cassette or CD player. Better yet, serenade each other.

stays open twelve hours a day to rent paddle boats, windsurfers, canoes, sailboats, and power boats for fishing and water skiing. Fishing guides are available with advance notice.

The resort also boasts a large multicourt outdoor tennis facility, an indoor tennis court, an archery range, shuffleboard, and a large lawn for other games. Bikes can be rented for riding on the trails, and horse stables provide scenic, guided forty-five minute rides. In the winter, cutter sleigh rides are available.

In the evening, if you still are itching for some action, you can watch the horse show at the Arrowwood stables, join a volleyball game, or roast some marshmallows at a bonfire on the beach. The Rafter's Lounge provides live entertainment on Fridays and Saturdays and Luigi's shows first-run movies and classic films every night of the week.

The management encourages guests to respect a 10:30 P.M. quiet time, so that those seeking a more peaceful evening are not unduly disturbed. Once visitors stay at Arrowwood they are likely to return; the resort enjoys 60 to 70 percent repeat business. One reason may be that Arrowwood is the only full-size resort to receive the AAA award for over thirteen years.

If you get the room with the double-sized wall of windows that overlook the lake, and there is a full moon or an electrical storm, you can pull back all the curtains and enjoy an evening of celestial light effects. This massive wall of glass lets you feel as though you are outside, without the worry of bugs or raindrops.

*Because there are so many water
opportunities, learn how to sail, fish, or
windsurf in advance. Lessons between
lovers can result in less than
a romantic experience.*

2100 ARROWWOOD LANE • P.O. BOX 639 • ALEXANDRIA

612-762-1124

Southern Minnesota

Along with the charming inns and restaurants described in this section, southern Minnesota offers a variety of natural settings—prairies, hardwood forests, lakes, and rivers—that offer both spectacular and subtle beauty.

You can enjoy them on an automobile trip, but for a closer look, try a bicycle ride along one of these trails.

Root River Trail

Visitors at Mrs. B's or the Victorian House in Lanesboro will enjoy the rolling hills and diverse scenery as they ride through the Root River valley.

Cannon Valley trail system

If the St. James Hotel is your destination and the bluff country is your choice, this trail follows the old Chicago Great Western Railroad line and a beautiful river.

Minnesota Valley Trail

Guests at Bluff Creek Inn will enjoy the Minnesota Valley Trail, which winds through state park and national wildlife refuge lands. The valley is a mix of woods and prairies, dry and wet, with easy pedaling.

DUNDAS

VICTORIAN HOME

QUIET EVENINGS AND GOURMET BREAKFASTS

Martin Oaks Bed and Breakfast

A stay at Martin Oaks Bed and Breakfast provides couples a beautiful historic home to relax in as well as a hostess who doubles as a professional storyteller. Owner Marie Gery grew up listening to the women in her family tell tales of her relatives and of the milling family who built the home in 1869. Marie weaves within her stories the rumors their small-town neighbors once spread about the inhabitants of the house, rumors that became myths as they grew along with the shrubbery and vines that almost obscured the house by the 1960s.

A well-to-do farmer's home with touches of Italianate and Victorian detail, Martin Oaks sits on a very large corner lot. The Gerys have bolstered the original flower beds and plan further expansion in years ahead. The house itself is continually filled with fresh-cut or dried flowers. Guests enter the home through a plant-filled foyer where baskets of floral potpourri fill the house with sweet smells. Dried-flower wreaths and swags hang on the walls and doors, and guests find more flowers in unexpected places.

A piano sits in the main floor's parlor, and the Gerys encourage their guests to play.

Of the three guest rooms, couples will want to choose one of the two with tall double beds. Beautifully stenciled flowers decorate the white walls of Sarah's Room and match the handmade reproduction of the Smithsonian Collection's Baltimore Bride quilt that covers the bed. Window shades and curtain tiebacks carry the stencil design throughout the room, and a small hand-hooked rug hangs on one wall. Floral wallpaper and antique furniture decorate the Martin Suite, the inn's largest guest room. Thick, plush carpeting covers the floor, and lace curtains let lots of bright light into the room.

The house is continually filled with fresh-cut or dried flowers.

When retiring for the night, guests in each room find their beds turned down and a dish of rich chocolate brownies on a table in the room. Fresh-brewed coffee set on a table in the area between the rooms greets them as they rise. While visitors must share the bathroom, the hosts provide thick terry robes for wandering the halls in modesty.

A sumptuous breakfast is served in the formal dining room at a table set with candles, silver, and china place settings. The meal may include a fresh fruit cup with colorful seasonal fruit drizzled with honey, fresh squeezed orange juice, grandiose muffins, fluffy Belgian waffles with apple butter and cinnamon syrup, and turkey ham or sausage.

In the warmer seasons, guests enjoy the comfort of a large front porch where they can sit back and listen to the breeze blow through the top of the big maple or chat with the owners about life in the little town of Dundas. A historic walking tour has been put together, and if she has the time, Marie will accompany guests on their tour, adding more detail and a storyteller's touch to the tour's informational narration.

**50
Ways
to
Lure your Lover**

*Find an old time
photography shop
and sit for a
period photo.*

If you visit on a summer weekend, you may have a chance to see the Dundas Dukes baseball team play on their own little field of dreams just down from the Martin Oaks. You may also wish to take a blanket and wander to the banks of the Cannon River just two blocks west to relax and imagine life one hundred years ago, when Dundas was a thriving milling community with grand plans for growth and development. Fate intervened when the mill burned down and a town four miles north began to prosper, allowing Dundas to keep the tranquility of the countryside to itself.

The peaceful little town inspires romance. Marie tells of one young couple who came to Dundas in search of a small, quaint church to be married in. They found an old stone Episcopal church built by the Archibald family more than one hundred years before. Marie called the post office to inquire about the church, and it so happened that the deaconess was picking up her mail at the time. She gladly showed the church to the couple, who quickly fell in love with the stone building and were married there soon after.

DUNDAS

507-645-4644

FARIBAULT

AN 1896 VICTORIAN GET-AWAY

Cherub Hill Bed and Breakfast

 he heavenly Cherub Hill Bed and Breakfast takes its name from the cherubs that grace the tiles surrounding its parlor fireplace. Owner Jean E. Cummings continues the angelic theme set by the inn's previous owners, who felt the name honored the Victorian home's original owner, Dr. Jonathon Noyes, the first superintendent of the School for the Deaf in Faribault and a man who dedicated his life to children. The cherub theme runs throughout the old house, each seraph acting as a little guardian angel to watch over all who visit the inn.

Stepping into the foyer of this 1896 house takes visitors back into the Victorian era. Former owners Kristi and Keith LeMieux worked very hard to restore this historic home and replicate the decor and setting of this period as closely as possible, and Jean strives to maintain and enhance their restoration.

Through patient research and snooping they discovered architect Olaf Hanson's original blueprints in ar-

chives at the School for the
Deaf. They also found information about the Noyes family in
the town library. For over sixty
years—and through four owners—the house remained in its
original condition. The fifth
owner, however, divided it into
apartments and unfortunately
removed some of the histori-
cally significant pieces.

> *Whisper love sonnets*
>
> *to each other as you*
>
> *enjoy the decadent*
>
> *chocolate treat you'll*
>
> *find on your pillow.*

But the house's guardian angels came to the rescue
when the LeMieuxs discovered several of the missing
doors, a fretwork arch, and a bedroom mirror in the attic
and basement of the home.

The four guest rooms—each named for a Noyes family member—occupy the second floor. Jonathon's Room,
complete with fireplace and dark, heavy wood furniture,
sits at the top of the deep rose-colored stenciled stairway. Its bathroom features a large claw-foot tub. White
wicker furniture and a white iron bed complement the
rich rose and paisley design of Elizabeth's Room. Named
for the good doctor's wife, it also offers an intimate little
parlor just off the bathroom.

The LeMieuxs named the room across the hall from
Elizabeth's in honor of the Noyes' daughter, Alice. While
its bath is down the hall, the large and airy forest green
room boasts a corner whirlpool jacuzzi that inspired one
guest to read Byron's poetry at the top of his lungs to his
wife during a weekend getaway. A brass bed with delicate
draped netting at the corners highlights the fourth room—
named for Alice's son, Noyes Bartlett. A faux marble floor

and a large whirlpool tub make its bathroom one of the most inviting in the inn.

Romance permeates your stay from the moment you arrive at Cherub Hill. Jean greets guests who check in between 4 and 6 P.M. with a complimentary tea in the front parlor. Sweets and fruit, crackers and tea, as well as a relaxed conversation with your hosts, create a pleasant introduction to your stay.

Visitors are welcome to stroll among the flower and herb gardens that surround the house or enjoy the view from the wide, covered front porch. On rainy days or after an afternoon visiting historic Faribault, guests will want to explore the house and its many antiques, particularly the Eastlake parlor set in the front room and the bustle bench in the entryway.

Served two ways, the inn's breakfast matches the splendor of the house. Guests can enjoy either a continental breakfast served to their rooms or a full meal in the dining room. The formal breakfast starts with fresh-squeezed orange juice, sliced fruits, and fresh-baked muffins before moving on to an elegant main course of eggs and potatoes. Coffee and tea are served as well.

When guests retire for the evening they find the bed covers turned down, a decadent chocolate treat on each pillow, and a petite book of Shakespeare's love sonnets resting beneath the bedside lamp. All these amenities—like tiny arrows from that romantic little cherub Cupid—combine to create a romantic mood that remains with you throughout your stay.

105 NW FIRST AVENUE • FARIBAULT

507-332-2024

ST. PETER
QUEEN ANNE STYLE
FOUR GUEST ROOMS

Park Row Bed & Breakfast

nn Burckhardt thinks of herself as your Aunt Harriet, a sweet, white-haired aunt, who leads you to the "bottomless" pineapple-shaped cookie jar as soon as you arrive. Ann has chosen the pineapple—a traditional colonial symbol for hospitality—as the theme for her Queen Anne style bed-and-breakfast. The house has a cheerful yellow exterior with lots of white gingerbread trim. Unlike most bed-and-breakfasts, Park Row has two of its four guest rooms on the ground floor, where they are accessible for guests who are unable to climb stairs. Each room is named for a different country, whose books, paintings, and memorabilia decorate the room.

On the main floor, a pair of pocket doors separate the parlor from the English Room, the house's largest guest room. A blue and white print border near the ceiling accents the room's Wedgwood blue walls. A large picture window faces the street, and above it a leaded glass window allows light to play off the ceiling and walls, surprising guests with colorful designs after the lights go out at night.

111

Antique furniture and headboards along with the ceramic teapots that top the dresser and recessed wall shelves add

to the room's English atmosphere. The French Room, also on the first floor, has a small blue and white pattern on the wallpaper and matching fabric on the bed skirt and window curtains. A white wrought iron and brass bed frame blends with French provincial picture frames, creating a mood so effective it prompted one young swain to write his memories in the room's journal in French. He concluded by saying that he would always think of the room he stayed in with his lady love as *la chambre d'amour*.

Guests access the rooms on the second floor by separate stairways. The most private guest room, the German Room, sits at the top of the front stairs and often houses honeymoon couples. Red, blue, and green flowered fabric accents the antique settee and queen-size bed that furnish the room. The rear staircase leads to the Norwegian room, decorated with flowered wallpaper, a blue headboard and dresser, and a dried flower wreath. The guests we spoke to found romance in this room through the nostalgia it evoked. Its slanted ceilings and wide-planked white wooden floor reminded one visitor of the room she grew up in, and the double-hung windows ventilated at the bottom took one man back to the farm of his youth.

Twin down-filled duvets enveloped in crisp white linen cover all the beds at Park Row, adding to the ambiance of an old European inn. Not many Americans know the comfort found in these lightweight yet warm bed coverings. Guests on each floor share common bathrooms, but the host provides robes for those who do not bring their own. Both bathrooms have tubs and showers. The tub on the second floor is six feet long with a wooden rim and brass shower fittings.

Owner Ann Burckhardt has written about food for the *Star Tribune* for over twenty years. Bookshelves in the living room and kitchen are packed with her collection of cookbooks, including many that she has edited, and her expertise is evident in the bed-and-breakfast's wonderful meals. Ann happily shares her favorite recipes with guests, and conversations around the dining room table during breakfast often last almost until lunchtime.

Since St. Peter is home to Gustavus Adolphus
College and just north of Mankato State
University, Park Row makes a great place
for parents to stay during a visit to
their college-aged children.

525 W. PARK ROW • ST. PETER

507-931-2495 FOR RESERVATIONS

PRESTON

FILLMORE COUNTY JAIL 1869-1971

JailHouse Historic Inn

If you consider yourself a prisoner of love jailed for committing crimes of the heart, the little town of Preston offers a place for you and your cellmate to allow love to bloom behind bars. There you will find the JailHouse Historic Inn, a beautifully restored Italianate building that *Minnesota Monthly* called "a bed-and-breakfast worth going to jail for."

A former mayor of Preston and president of the Fillmore County Historic Society saved the building, which served as the Fillmore County jail from 1869 until 1971, from destruction in an attempt to transform it into a county museum. While the museum plans failed, his efforts did place the structure on the National Historic Register. This reprieve gave the structure another chance at life, which came in 1989 when another local man bought the building and converted it to an inn. Marc and Jeanne Sather purchased the inn from its renovator just before it opened. Moving from San Francisco during a holiday blizzard, the Sathers arrived at their new establishment at 5 P.M. New

Year's Eve. Their first guests arrived fifteen minutes later.

Since the Sathers' arrival, the inn has seen more renovations and additions. The interior, completely gutted during reconstruction, was refitted with all the original materials the builders could salvage. The house's woodwork stands as a testament to both fine craftsmanship and the hardwood forests that grow in this area. Where the floorboards had to be replaced, the newer wood was distressed to match the older boards.

The majority of the rooms take their names from sheriffs who served in the building, beginning with H. C. Gullickson in 1869 and ending with Carl Fann in 1971, while the names of the rest, such as the Amish Room, the Oriental Room, and the Fan Room, reflect the interior design.

Locally acquired antique furnishings add to the jail's connection with local history. The long copper bathtub in the Amish Room, for instance, came from a farm home in nearby Harmony. The Oriental Room's marble fireplace with a black and pink splatter pattern is an Eastlake design, while the master bedroom's fireplace mantel came from one of the homes of the Mayos, founders of Rochester's famous medical facilities. The master bedroom also boasts a huge, clawless porcelain tub weighing 968 pounds. All the antique bed frames, many of which are also Eastlake design, have been

> *While each room has its own unique charm, most guests want to visit the Cell Block. No prisoner ever enjoyed such a comfortable cell.*

modified to accept queen-size mattresses.

While each room at the JailHouse Historic Inn has its own unique charm, most guests want to visit the Cell Block. While its blue-grey iron bars remain in place, no prisoner ever enjoyed such a comfortable cell. Two queen-size beds have replaced uncomfortable bunks, and a large jacuzzi sits next to the window. As in each of the inn's rooms, thick terry robes rest on the tub for the use of guests. The room also now allows access to an upper-level porch, an option not available when the room played host to criminal elements. While incarceration may not inspire romance, the Cell Block ranks high in originality

Guests can find beverages and snacks in the large kitchen area next to the front sitting room. Breakfast is served in the lower dining area, where skylights covering the ceiling allow bright light to fill the room. A huge fireplace sits along one wall, adding warmth and a romantic mood in cooler seasons. The hosts will serve dinner to guests on holidays or special events, such as weddings or reunions, and don't forget to ask about the jail break.

109 HOUSTON STREET • PRESTON

507-765-2181

NORTHFIELD, ON CANNON RIVER

HISTORIC RED BRICK HOTEL

The Archer House

he Archer House, perched along the Cannon River in Northfield, first opened in 1877 as an elegant and fashionable inn. The years since have seen owners come and go, and sadly, the beautiful structure gradually fell into a state of disrepair. Dallas Haas, who had renovated buildings next door to the hotel and who owned some of the nearby shops, rescued the Archer House when he reluctantly took over its ownership. Although the building was a mess when Haas purchased it, his effort to reconstruct, renovate, and redecorate the Archer House has brought it back to life in all its past glory.

The red brick, Italianate style building has clean white trim around the windows and along its full-length wooden front porch. The reception area's walls glow with wainscoting of dark, rich wood, stenciled designs edge the walls, and the original tin ceiling gleams with a fresh coat of white paint. The dark pine furniture, detailed with carvings of pine cones and needles and upholstered with maroon and green plaid fabric, accents the wainscoting.

117

The Archer House's thirty-eight rooms, including nineteen suites, are spread between the second and third floors. Guests choose from rooms with a view of the river or of the hill leading to nearby Carlton College. The names of the rooms relate to either their decor or the area's history, and all have many personal touches, including country wreaths, bouquets, dolls, stuffed animals, and paintings. Guests find their towels held in unusual containers. If you see something you really like, you can purchase it; the Archer House makes all the artwork, decorative items, and pine furnishings available for sale. In this way, guests can find articles for their homes and the inn can continually change the decor as items are purchased and replaced.

Some of the rooms offer a cozy escape for couples, with just enough room for the queen-size bed, a small dresser, and a chair, plus a bathroom in the corner. Other rooms have larger sitting areas, and a few, such as the Anniversary Room and the Manor House, are full suites with large bedrooms and sitting areas.

The Anniversary Room, awash in white lace and flowers, will bring back wedding memories.

Careful attention has been paid to the furnishings in each room, many of which inspire romance. The bed in Summer Haus, with its bent-willow headboard shaped like a heart and handmade quilt, invites couples to linger under the covers just a while longer each morning. The wedding ring quilt covering Little Women's white iron and brass bed reminds married couples of their love. Both the Jefferson Room and Willi's View come complete with a small wet bar and a jacuzzi tub in the bathroom.

Couples can even find a north-woods escape in this majestic nine-teenth-century hotel. Memories, an especially fun room, has walls and ceilings paneled in wood shaped to look like logs. A stuffed toy moose head hangs over the bed, and old cross-country skis, ice skates, and bamboo fishing poles complete the tableau. The bed's quilt, pure Minne-sota, accents the room with appli-qued loons, ladyslippers, and chicka-dees, and an assortment of large and small pillows fill half of the bed. A mirror set inside a horse collar hangs on one wall, and the bathroom has an eye-opening red jacuzzi.

Located on the street side, the Bridal Room offers hospitality for newlyweds unconcerned with the view. The room centers around a high four-poster bed with lace curtains; a pair of teddy bears in wedding attire sit in the middle of the bed, sur-rounded by a mountain of pillows. In the bathroom, folded towels fill an antique wooden basket and a large jacuzzi tub runs along one of the walls. Couples not-so-fresh from the

50
Ways
to
Lure your Lover

Create a romantic

scrapbook filled

with ticket stubs,

napkins, menus,

notes, postcards—

little items to

remind each other

of your romance.

altar will enjoy the Anniversary Room, a large suite awash in white lace and flowers. Its bathroom, separated from the bedroom by a partial wall, also boasts a large jacuzzi perched two steps above the floor.

Guests will enjoy dining at restaurants near the hotel and visiting the shops that dot the historic town of Northfield. The hotel has been in great demand since the Mall of America opened in Bloomington, so be sure to make reservations. Ask for a room on the river side.

Guests staying in a room with a whirlpool receive hand-painted wine glasses stenciled with their names plus a bottle of champagne or nonalcoholic beverage with the Archer House name and picture gracing the bottle.

Visit the Archer House and attend the St. Olaf Christmas concert, a magnificent holiday celebration.

212 DIVISION STREET • NORTHFIELD

507-645-5661

The Anderson House

he Mississippi sweeps past Wabasha, carrying the speedboats and barges of our modern world as well as memories of slower steam-powered craft of the nineteenth century. While highways and rail systems have moved the commerce of transport further from town, the brick buildings along Main Street and the large, wooden gabled homes of the surrounding neighborhoods remind visitors of bustling days gone by. Two blocks west of the river stands The Anderson House, the oldest operating hotel in Minnesota. Its sturdy brick walls and white window frames beckon the romantic to enter, just as they did over one hundred years ago.

The Anderson family has owned the inn since 1896 and has maintained a strong tradition of hospitality throughout changing times. As guests check in at the front desk, they find an ever-filled cookie jar the clerk encourages them to delve into. The stairs leading to the second- and third-floor guest rooms creak a bit, and the carpeted hallways have a slight rise and fall reminiscent of the current of the nearby river. Visitors can almost feel the presence of the many other travelers who have passed through the corridors of the old hotel.

A heated brick wrapped in a quilted liner will warm your toes on a cold winter night.

The pleasantly decorated rooms have an old-fashioned feel, with tiny flower print wallpaper and well-used antiques, many from the early days of the hotel's operation. Some rooms have private baths, while others share a bath located on each floor. Through gradual renovations that combine some rooms to create suites, the number of private baths increases each year. This National Historic Landmark offers unique services rarely found in modern hotels, such as shoe shining. On cold winter nights the service staff delivers a hot brick wrapped in a quilted liner to help warm the foot of the bed.

Another unique service stems from a long-ago visit by a sickly guest who stayed at the hotel for an extended period because of frequent medical visits in nearby Rochester. After he expressed a longing for companionship, one of the owners brought a family housecat to stay with the lonely guest. A tradition was born. Room 19 now houses anywhere from nine to twelve cats available on a daily basis as company for the hotel's guests. Visitors need only let the desk know which cat they'd like and it will soon arrive at their door with food and a litter box. The cats have mellow temperaments and are accustomed to visiting with many different people.

Guests at the Anderson House enjoy the hotel's full hospitality only if they take time to dine in the hotel's restaurant. Waitresses dress in red checked uniforms with Dutch-styled hats, complementing the food's emphasis on Pennsylvania Dutch recipes, a carryover from Grandma Anderson's heritage. The kitchen has made a name for itself with its supersized caramel and cinnamon rolls, baked fresh every morning and served piping hot with icing dripping down the sides. Couples can share one individual serving and have plenty to eat.

The expansive evening meals begin with a tray covered with several varieties of freshly baked breads. A typical tray may include blueberry streusel, black walnut bread, cheese bread, rye rolls, and lemon bread. The wonderful homemade soups and pies all start from long-kept family recipes. Every Friday, the restaurant offers a salad bar and fish buffet featuring walleye, cod, and shrimp, and Saturday evenings feature barbecue as the specialty.

Plan your visit to The Anderson House: it operates only on weekends from November 1 until April 1, but remains open every day for the rest of the year.

50 Ways to Lure your Lover

Find a relaxing spot on a river bluff and read to one another from a collection of Mark Twain stories.

R o m a n c i n g

*A man came into the Anderson House with
an engagement ring that he wanted to
present to his girlfriend in a special way. He
asked the front desk clerk to help, and she
had the box wrapped in aluminum foil and
hidden inside the young woman's piece of
pie; whipped cream concealed the treasure.
The second plunge of her fork produced a
look of bewilderment as it struck the hidden
treasure. Both the waitress and boyfriend
had a difficult time keeping a straight face.*

*If you can arrange to arrive by boat, it will
add to the sense of history and adventure.*

333 WEST MAIN STREET • WABASHA

612-565-4524 • 800-535-5467

NEW PRAGUE

BAVARIAN STYLE INN

THREE DINING ROOMS, ELEVEN GUEST ROOMS

Schumacher's New Prague Hotel

If you've ever dreamed of taking a European vacation but didn't have the time or the money, Schumacher's New Prague Hotel makes a wonderful surrogate getaway for couples in love with the romance of a trip abroad. Schumacher's has been deemed a "Romantik Hotel" by the European Association of Inns and Hotels, an international organization of unique and historic hostelries. The honor of belonging to this group requires a high level of service and quality, and the New Prague Hotel was the first in the United States to become a member. Owner and head chef John Schumacher sets high standards for himself, his staff, and his establishment. According to him, "You can't get any more romantic than this place." He describes the atmosphere at the Hotel as *gemutlichkeit*, German for "warmth and comfort." With three distinctive dining rooms and a dark-paneled pub, the hotel offers a full-service retreat where every customer receives royal treatment.

Since 1974, John has gradually remodeled and

renovated the century-old hotel, reducing the thirteen original guest rooms to eleven larger, more comfortable rooms. All of the rooms have large whirlpool bathtubs, and seven have gas fireplaces. John and his wife Kathleen have worked diligently to decorate the rooms, each named for a month of the year, with furnishings from Central Europe, creating a decor that gives the hotel the feel of a Bavarian country house. The September room, for instance, has a hand-carved Bavarian pine double bed, folk-painted furniture, and a wooden ceiling finished in a European style. In the March room, pink chandeliers and wall sconces exemplify Czech glass work.

While each room features different colors and furniture, all receive the same attention to detail, including German eiderdown-filled comforters, Czech and Austrian bed linens, and down pillows plumped up like white Hershey kisses. Guests find a half bottle of German wine with two glasses waiting on a shelf and special, gold foil-wrapped chocolates tucked under the pillow in the custom of Central European inns. They will not, however, find TVs in their rooms, although the rooms do have stereos to add soft, soothing music to their retreat.

Guests receive royal treatment in a relaxing, warm, and comfortable atmosphere.

Opening a guest room door brings the delicious aromas drifting up from the kitchen, drawing guests to the dining rooms below. John ties his internationally known culinary skills with the

Central European atmosphere of the hotel and the ethnic background of the local community, resulting in a extensive menu that satisfies the eclectic tastes of adventuresome diners. John insists on making everything from scratch, quite a task for a menu with fifty-five entrees. The menu features many wild game selections, such as quail, rabbit, pheasant, venison, and roast duck. While a variety of "heart healthy" entrees have been added to the menu for those who must have low-fat and low-cholesterol meals, passing up the gravies, cream sauces, dumplings, Wiener schnitzel, and spaetzle takes a great deal of will power.

John dedicates an entire page of his menu to desserts, including tortes, strudels, and cheesecakes. The most well-known and sought-after Czech treat on the menu is the kolache, a sweet roll filled with apricot, prune, or poppy seed filling, made at 3:30 A.M. every day by local women whose families have been making them for generations.

The decor of the hotel's three dining rooms complements the efforts of the kitchen staff to create a complete old-world setting. In the Garden Room, for instance, the glow of the fireplace reflects off 150-year-old Bavarian pine wainscoting and windows open onto a garden. Little strings

50
Ways
to
Lure your Lover

Families with children might trade baby-sitting once a year to allow each couple time for a romantic retreat.

of white lights sparkle like fireflies among the shrubbery, and grapevines climb and twist their way among the brick pillars and wooden fence. The warmth of the room is enhanced by the quiet candlelit tables, creating a perfect setting for romance.

The hotel's popularity continues to grow, so you will need reservations. Many guests return each year to their favorite room, while others choose to sample a variety, so call ahead to make sure your favorite is available. A stay at the New Prague Hotel gives you a taste of a European vacation without ever leaving the country.

212 WEST MAIN ST. • NEW PRAGUE

612-758-2133

Saying "I love you"
GERMAN
Ich liebe dich

LANESBORO

PATIO AND HERB GARDEN

FRESH REGIONAL CUISINE

Mrs. B's Historic Lanesboro Inn and Restaurant, Ltd.

On the main street of the sleepy river town of Lanesboro stands a stately limestone building. Once a furniture store and later a funeral parlor, the building has been transformed into Mrs. B's Historic Lanesboro Inn and Restaurant, Ltd., welcoming visitors to a restful and relaxing retreat in one of Minnesota's most beautiful river valleys.

The inn, named for a former owner, has been under new management since early 1991. None of the amenities have changed, although the owners, Mimi Abell and Bill Sermeus, have added a patio and herb garden at the back of the building. Old barn wood and brick define the area, and scattered seating allows guests to sit back, inhale the sweet and subtle scent of herbs, and listen to bird song.

Lace curtains frame the building's gracefully arched door and a pair of tall windows. Inside, a high ceiling and dark blue flowered wallpaper greet guests in the sitting room. A fireplace set in one wall gives off glowing heat in the winter, while in warmer weather the room becomes a cool, quiet refuge where guests can sit and read, play one of the many games found on the shelves, or enjoy the tea service on Friday and Saturday afternoons at three.

Thick red Oriental rugs cushion the entry and the halls and stairs leading to the inn's ten guest rooms on the first and second floors. While rooms tend to be smaller than in some other bed-and-breakfasts, their attractive and comfortable appointments more than make up for their size. Natural country-Victorian motifs, including beds either fully or partially canopied, match the building's architectural style. One room features a Norwegian sleigh bed, another a Norwegian cupboard bed, and each has its own private bath. During summer visits, guests should request one of the three rooms with access to a balcony sitting area, where they can soak up sunshine and listen to the Root River tumble past.

The inn's talented chef maintains its reputation for delicious food. Using as much local produce as possible, both wild and garden grown, the menu features the freshest regional cuisine. In the spring, entrees may include sauteed morel mushrooms, steamed asparagus, black walnut torte, or plum blossom ice cream. Each meal starts with a soup and salad course followed by the main entree, with side dishes offering a variety of vegetables. The menu varies nightly and offers a choice of desserts and wine and a fine selection of locally brewed beers. Guests who enjoy a nightcap simply must try Mrs. B's Bedtime Bump, a family recipe guaranteed to send you to bed with a sleepy smile. When you wake, a hearty country breakfast—included with your room—waits downstairs.

Meals are served family style, so a couple may be

seated with one or two other couples at a table. The food and friendly service make introductions to one another easy. There are, however, a few tables just for two, so request one of these if you prefer private conversation with your partner.

While the inn offers pure relaxation, Lanesboro itself and the surrounding river valley cry out for exploration. Stroll the sidewalks of the main street's three or four blocks and visit its antique shops, or stop at the corner drugstore and enjoy a treat from the soda fountain. Visitors who enjoy the outdoors will want to take a hike or a bike ride on the Root River Trail in the wooded bluffs behind town. Winter finds the trail groomed for cross-country skiing. Just down the street from the inn, an outfitter rents canoes, bikes, and fishing gear and provides a shuttle service for canoeists. A day spent in the beautiful outdoors of the Root River Valley makes the return to the inn for a meal or an overnight stay a complete and satisfying romantic escape.

50 Ways
to
Lure your Lover

Two straws in a single chocolate soda will bring back memories of teenage romance.

101 PARKWAY • LANESBORO
507-467-2154 • 800-657-4710

RED WING

HISTORIC BRICK HOTEL WITH VERANDA CAFE, ENGLISH PUB

St. James Hotel

 he town of Red Wing grew out of river commerce during the last half of the nineteenth century. The town boomed as riverboats and barges made their way up and down the Mississippi carrying visitors and goods to and from the south. Nothing reflects the history of the town more than the St. James Hotel, a wonderful red brick building built in 1875 on a prominent corner of Red Wing's Main Street.

For seventy years, one family owned and operated the hotel, and it enjoyed a reputation for quality and service. But time took its toll on the building and the family, and the hotel fell into a state of disrepair. The Red Wing Shoe Company purchased the hotel in 1977 and executed a complete and detailed restoration. The new owners recognized the historic value of the building and its connection to the Mississippi River. Today, a couple wishing to escape from the pressures of today's fast-paced world can step back into the quiet, elegant days of Victorian riverboating when they plan a retreat at the St. James.

Couples staying at the St. James can enjoy a completely self-contained escape. Port of Red Wing Restaurant, located on the lower level, offers American and continental cuisine in a rathskeller setting. The Veranda Cafe on the second floor has a bright, many-windowed breezeway with a great view of the river. The fourth floor boasts an English pub with stained glass windows and appropriately dark wood paneling and beams. A library sitting room off the lobby offers guests a chance to relax in leather wing chairs next to a crackling fire. Guests can also stroll through the hotel's own set of shops, browsing in the great little bookstore, the country crafts and floral boutique, three clothing boutiques, and the card and gift shop that greet visitors as they enter the Main Street doorway.

The dark wood paneling and thick carpeting give a sense of elegance and graciousness, and the single, small elevator by the front desk reminds guests of the hotel's age.

In the new wing the atmosphere suggests a paddle wheeler's staterooms. Each room has wide bay windows providing a nice view of the riverfront.

The St. James's guest rooms take their names from some of the riverboats that worked the Mississippi in the past century, such as the *Lady*, the *Mark Twain*, the *Commodore*, the *Mississippi Queen*, and the *War Eagle*. A photo of the boat for which the room was named hangs in each room, and high ceilings grace the halls and rooms of the original building. While the rooms have undergone remodeling, they retain unusual angles that give them a quaint feeling. Each features antique-styled furnishings and wallpaper in rich tones of maroon, green, and blue. Beautiful handmade quilts made by local women, including some from the Amish community, cover each bed. In order to protect them, a maid comes by each evening and removes them, returning them the next day when the rooms are cleaned.

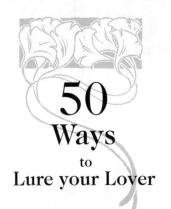

50 Ways
to
Lure your Lover

Chose a retreat
your partner will
enjoy. If she is an
angler, look for a
fishing lodge. If he
loves opera, plan
an evening at
the Ordway.

In the new wing, a locked door on each floor restricts entrance to those with room keys. Ornate wooden archways lead guests through the hallway, and the walls are papered in period coverings with borders at the top. Electric glass lanterns and antique-framed Victorian paintings hang on the wall, providing a sense of being on board a paddle wheeler. You can almost hear the river passing by. Each room has wide bay windows providing a nice view of the riverfront.

An indoor escape seems especially appealing to Minnesotans in the middle of winter, when the windchill factor drops and the roads turn icy. For couples interested in a winter getaway, the St. James offers its special Winterlude package from November through April.

Attention to details adds to the romance at
this historic hotel. In your room, you will find
a small bottle of champagne (or nonalcoholic
Catawba juice) resting in ice in a cut glass
bowl, and on the bedside table a tiny golden
treasure chest holds fine chocolates
made especially for the St. James.

Amtrak provides passenger service to Red
Wing. The train stops at a small station just
below the hotel. Taking the train will begin
your passage back in time. You might also
bring one of Mark Twain's riverboat stories
and share a page or two to create the
proper mood to go with the setting.

406 MAIN ST. • RED WING

612-388-2846 • 800-252-1875

LANESBORO
GOURMET FRENCH RESTAURANT

The Victorian House of Lanesboro French Restaurant

One doesn't expect to find a gourmet French restaurant in the sleepy little river town of Lanesboro, but the service and food at the Victorian House live up to the description.

The house, a big white Victorian, has lots of gingerbread detail common to that style. After years of polishing, the entryway's deep brown paneling glows with a warm patina, giving guests the feeling of entering a great aunt's home rather than a restaurant. Owner Sonja Venant personally greets visitors and seats them at a table in one of three intimate dining rooms. The low lighting of the Victorian-decorated rooms creates an intimate setting, but remains bright enough to allow you to fully appreciate the beautifully prepared dishes. Piano music, often that of Sonja herself, plays softly in the background.

Sonja owns the restaurant with her husband Jean Claude, a chef she met while both worked for a cruise line. He was born in Nice, France, but grew up in Alsace-Lorraine. Sonja hails from the Lanesboro area; when both decided they'd seen enough of the sea, they chose to settle on dry land in Sonja's home area, and French cuisine came to Lanesboro.

The menu offers five or six entrees, and the choices change every six weeks. They use local produce as much as possible and have a special supplier for herbs. The food is rich and filling, but wise diners will want to leave room for Sonja's Chocolate Sin, a decadent dessert consisting of vanilla ice cream rolled up in a crepe, drenched in deep, dark chocolate sauce, and topped with whipped cream and a slice of kiwi. Special cakes can be ordered for anniversaries if you let them know ahead of time.

Beautifully polished woodwork and careful attention to detail are reminiscent of your great aunt's well cared for home.

Sonja complements her husband's delicious French food with outstanding service. At the request of guests, she takes time to describe the menu and help select a wine to accompany dinner. After the main entree, Sonja brings out a bottle of rose-scented water and sprinkles it on your hands. And guests with the willpower to forgo dessert receive a special Love Bird post dinner mint, a piece of rich chocolate embossed with a heart and a dove. Guests at the Victorian House can relax and enjoy their evening out without worrying that their hosts would prefer them to eat quickly and make room for another seating. As far as Sonja and Jean Claude are concerned, the table belongs to the guests for the entire evening.

Folks outside the Lanesboro area should plan a visit
to the Victorian House well ahead. The restaurant's doors
open only Wednesday through Sunday and remain closed
during February and March. Their busiest season begins
in May and runs through the summer.

709 S. PARKWAY • LANESBORO

507-467-3457

HOURS: WEDNESDAY–SUNDAY, 5:30 P.M.—CLOSING

STAY AS LONG AS YOU WISH

CLOSED DURING FEBRUARY AND MARCH

CALL FOR RESERVATIONS

Minnesota

The North Shore

Couples are enticed by the cozy retreats along Lake Superior's North Shore, but they enjoy them even more if they have first spent a day in the outdoors. Active and quiet pastimes await visitors to northern Minnesota. Consider a hike or a restful time to observe the natural world as you plan your trip for two.

Active hikes

Discover Minnesota's tallest waterfall at Tettegouche State Park.

Hike the Cascade River and enjoy the breathtaking view of waterfalls and rock walls.

Quiet contemplation

Watch the waves roll in on Minnesota Point in Duluth or the North Shore's Shovel Point.

Share the excitement of the annual hawk migration at Duluth's Hawk Ridge in September.

Sit among the rocks of the St. Louis River in Jay Cooke State Park and watch the river roll through a maze of slate and graywacke.

Romancing

LUTSEN, ON THE NORTH SHORE

COTTAGES WITH KITCHENS

Solbakken Resort

Solbakken Resort lies almost hidden along Lake Superior's North Shore, but couples on a getaway weekend won't want to miss it: its unassuming cabins make a perfect stop for romance. The resort includes a motel, cabins, two larger homes, and a rebuilt version of the old Sawbill Lodge, which reflects the history and rugged architecture of the north woods. Owners Bill and Beth Blank go out of their way to make a stay at Solbakken a wonderful experience, and even their cats, Goldie and Pumpkin—two immense balls of fur often found sleeping near the registration area—greet visitors as they check in.

Each of the six cabins has a fully equipped kitchen, bedrooms, and bath. Most important, each of the cabins feels like it belongs on the North Shore. They're simple, cozy, lived-in cottages furnished comfortably and separated enough from one another to be private. Each offers access to a piece of shoreline, adding to the sense of romance of the North Shore setting. While guests can find great restaurants in nearby Grand Marais and Lutsen, the cabins' full kitchens offer an opportunity for truly romantic visitors to whip up a special candlelit dinner for two or a hearty breakfast to start a day of outdoor adventure.

50 Ways
to
Lure your Lover

Share the plea-sures of cooking as well as the joys of eating.

Guests at Solbakken—which is open year round—will find a great variety of activities depending on the season. In the winter, some of the very best cross-country skiing in the Midwest lies just across the road in an elaborate system of North Shore ski trails. This trail system offers lodge-to-lodge options as well as many variations of circles and loops that bring skiers back to where they started. The trails rank from very easy flats to downhill thrills. The Blanks know the trails well and help visitors find the ones that best suit their skill level, available time, and desired skiing experience. One trail starting behind Cascade Park runs downhill for half a day. Skiers can park their car just outside of the park and the Blanks will provide a shuttle service to the beginning of the trail. It's a challenging and exhilarating trip that leaves skiers satisfied and filled with great memories of the day.

Summer offers romantics a walk along the lakeshore, in one of the nearby state parks, and along the Lake Superior Hiking Trail. Taking along a picnic lunch for a hike or a mountain bike run through the trails provides a great opportunity for a romantic rest during a day of exploration and discovery. In the fall, the North Shore draws visitors like a

Saying "I love you"
SWEDISH
Jeg alska dig

magnet when the colors of autumn set the hillsides ablaze in oranges, yellows, and reds. Spring is cool, often fogbound, and quiet—the easiest time to get a booking. Summer through winter, Solbakken—especially busy on weekends—often finds its cabins booked months in advance.

On the rocks in front of the cabins watch the sun dance on the lake or the fog roll in across the rocks. Listen to the gulls, immersing yourself in seaside images.

Solbakken allows small fires to be built on the rocky shoreline. Check with them about the location, and make sure that your fire is small and you clean up afterwards. It's hard to beat the sound of waves, the night sky filled with the northern lights, and a crackling fire to snuggle by.

HCR 3 • BOX 170 • LUTSEN
218-663-7566 • 800-435-3950

$\mathcal{N}$aniboujou $\mathcal{L}$odge

hen its original owners began building Naniboujou Lodge in the 1920s, they envisioned an exclusive, private club where socialites and celebrities could escape the heat and congestion of the east and west coasts for the fresh, pine-scented air of the north woods. Indeed, with charter members such as Babe Ruth, Jack Dempsey, and Ring Lardner, those plans seemed assured of success. Unfortunately, the Depression hit soon after the lodge opened its doors, and the club gradually fell into financial trouble—the dream faded, and Naniboujou was sold.

Luckily, even over decades and through various owners, the Main Lodge remains in its original condition, protected now by its listing on the National Register of Historic Places. Old architectural drawings that hang on the walls show an immense lodge with wings extending out in four directions, eight tennis courts on the lawn in front of the beach, a golf course, a promenade, and bathing cabanas.

146

While the entire plan never saw completion, the facilities remain impressive. The doors of the Main Lodge open into the Great Hall, an incredible room with magnificent multicolored frescoes based on Cree culture covering its walls and high, soaring ceiling. The hall, now used as a dining room, also boasts Minnesota's largest native rock fireplace. The fireplace—made of stones arranged in a beautiful pattern—weighs two hundred tons and measures thirty by eighty feet, nearly covering an entire wall.

Two wings of guests rooms—each renovated to include a private bath—extend from the Main Lodge. The rooms have been restored using the original colors and decor. In the south wing's rooms—smaller than the north's—rich wood paneling covers the walls, and all the lodge's rooms have double beds. Some rooms have a fireplace or lakeside view to make a stay at the lodge even more enjoyable.

Since the rooms lack large sitting areas, guests find further comfort in the brightly lit Arrowhead Room, a solarium with soft, peach-colored walls and comfortable sofas and chairs arranged in individual seating clusters. Windows provide a view of Lake Superior's great blue expanse on one side and the colorful Grand Hall on the other.

50 Ways to Lure your Lover

Those who enjoy a quiet rest will find Adirondack chairs to sit on while reading in the sun or watching the waves roll and tumble over the rocky shoreline.

Music plays softly in the background, so that the sound of the lake's waves and the bird calls seem like part of the composition. A TV with VCR, an upright piano, and a variety of games allow guests to entertain themselves when the weather outside keeps them indoors.

When the weather agrees, however, guests enjoy the abundance of natural beauty surrounding the lodge. A long cobblestone beach runs along Lake Superior, the Brule River flows just south, and Judge C. R. Magney State Park lies just across the road, offering guests ample places for walks and exploration. Those who enjoy a quiet rest will find Adirondack chairs to sit on while reading in the sun or simply watching the endless procession of waves roll in and tumble over the rocky shoreline.

Saying "I love you"
OJIBWA
Keen aetah k'bishiigaenimin

As a reminder of Naniboujou's prestigious history, the lodge's friendly and accommodating staff presents an afternoon tea, serving scones, sandwiches, and tea on pink and white patterned china between 3 and 5 P.M. Choosing to have tea naturally delays the evening meal, but guests won't want to forgo it completely. The dinner menu—with artwork taken from the original 1928 club membership booklet—offers a pleasing mix of fresh fish and deliciously-prepared meats, as well as many fresh fruits and vegetables. Guests enjoy meals while flames crackle in the fireplace and a hint of wood smoke drifts by.

The lodge remains open from mid-May until the

end of October, and for cozy winter weekends from the end of December until mid-March.

The Naniboujou takes its name from an impish Indian spirit, a trickster and a man-god who taught by experience.

The Anishinabe word for the relationship between a man and a woman is weedjeewaugun, meaning "companion on the path of life."

HC 80 • BOX 505 • GRAND MARAIS

218-387-2688

149

LUTSEN

SCANDINAVIAN SKI LODGE

GUEST ROOMS, CABINS

$\mathcal{L}$utsen $\mathcal{R}$esort and $\mathcal{S}$ea $\mathcal{V}$illas

While Lutsen Resort remains open year round, during the winter months, when ice begins to form on Lake Superior and snow covers the forested hillsides, the facility comes to life with all the charm of a true Scandinavian ski lodge. The Scandinavian atmosphere is in keeping with the resort's history. Original owner Charles A. Nelson immigrated to the United States in 1881 from Sweden and worked as a fisherman, tugboat captain, logger, and trapper along Superior's North Shore. His knowledge of the coastline convinced him to purchase and settle on property at the mouth of the Poplar River. Over the years he brought his brothers and parents to Minnesota and together they established the family resort business.

The main lodge faces a stretch of cobblestone beach along Lake Superior. Its sturdy pine timbers—cut from the surrounding forests—glow with the reflected flames of a huge fireplace, around which guests read, relax, and visit with one another. The second floor houses guest rooms simply furnished in a north-country cabin style, complete with wood paneling; lakeside rooms offer the best view. The resort recently unveiled new red pine log cabins with full kitchens in a sheltered woods along the shoreline, perfect for couples wishing a more secluded spot.

The best times at Lutsen involve outdoor activities. Guests can downhill ski at the nearby Lutsen Mountains Ski Area, which boasts some of the longest runs in the state, not to mention a view unmatched by any other ski area. As you look east from the top of its runs the great expanse of Lake Superior fades into the horizon.

For those who prefer nordic to alpine skiing, the North Shore Ski Trail—which includes 215 kilometers of groomed trail with varying degrees of difficulty—runs through the resort's property. At the request of guests, resort staff members will help tailor a cross-country tour for guests based on their abilities and will shuttle them to the trailhead. For a combination of downhill and cross-country, the trail from the top of Oberg Mountain offers 15 to 18 kilometers of combined skiing, most of it downhill. For those who don't like to climb, a gondola shuttles skiers to the top of Moose Mountain. The resort also rents cross-country equipment and offers introductory lessons.

50 Ways
to
Lure your Lover

Share a leisurely bath time that includes champagne, bubble bath, candles, and Handel's Water Music. Spare the bubble bath if you're using a whirlpool!

Snowmobilers also find groomed trails nearby. For those visiting during warmer seasons, Lutsen's new eighteen-hole championship golf course, sea kayaking facilities, and mountain bike tours offer hours of entertainment and exercise.

Saying "I love you"
ICELANDIC
Eg elska big

After a day in the clean, crisp north-country air, guests can soak their tired muscles in the resort's large, heated swimming pool and sauna or catch their breath in the Lodge Bar. The bar features "Polar Bear Wind Chill Warmers," an assortment of hot cocktails and alcohol-free drinks—such as the "Lutsen's Hot Banana Split" and the "Swedish Warm Body"—designed to warm the insides and ease any tightness that has set in from the day's endeavors.

Enjoy the bar, but don't drown your appetite. The dining room offers a satisfying way to quell hunger developed during the day's endeavors. Subdued lighting in the large room causes the wood to glow in golden tones, creating the relaxing, romantic atmosphere of a northern European getaway. The menu is standard American, with plenty of beef and wonderful fresh fish, including, of course, Lake Superior trout.

While fantastic skiing abounds in and around Lutsen Resort, guests will find a great time during any season. During the summers, Lutsen enjoys cool breezes off Lake Superior, and later the changing leaves of autumn set the surrounding forests ablaze with color.

In the early years, before Highway 61
reached along the shore, guests arrived by
boat and could only visit during the summer
months when the lake was ice free.

HIGHWAY 61 • LUTSEN

218-663-7212 • 800-258-8736

Duluth Hot Spots

Canal Park

The area surrounding Duluth's canal and its famous Aerial Lift Bridge was brought back to life during the 1980s. Its three lighthouses and marine museum take visitors back to days gone by, and a walk along the canal provides a close look at the big ships. Stop in the DeWitt-Seitz marketplace and browse through the shops, Eat at the Lake Avenue Cafe, try the Taste of Saigon for Vietnamese cuisine, or stop next door for southwestern fare at Little Angie's. Just down the block, the Blue Note Café offers wonderful espresso, cappuccino, latte, and imported coffee blends, occasionally accompanied by a live jazz combo. And, of course, there's always Grandma's. Canal Park Drive is also home to antique stores and other unique shops. Couples can even top off a romantic evening with a ride in a fringed surrey. If you want to get out on the water, try a sailboat charter or take a Vista Fleet day or night harbor cruise.

Fitger's complex

The Fitger's complex centers around a landmark brewery that has been converted into shop space. Inside, a hotel, a coffee shop, two restaurants, a nightclub, and a variety of shops make a great escape on rainy days or nights. Several wonderful places to dine, including Sir Benedict's, the Pickwick, and Hacienda Del Sol, lie only a brief walk away. The Malt Shoppe next door to the old Brewery is a must stop on warm summer evenings.

The Lakewalk

The most romantic way to get from Canal Park to the Fitger's complex is a stroll along the Lakewalk. The pathway, which includes a boardwalk for walking and a paved path for bicycles and roller blades, stretches along Lake Superior from the canal, past Fitger's, through Lief Erickson Park, and up the shore for several miles.

Minnesota Point

This extension of land separates the St. Louis River harbor from Lake Superior and provides one of the longest and most beautiful sand beaches in the Midwest, perfect for long walks, sunbathing, and—when it's not too cold—a swim in the world's largest freshwater lake. The beach also makes a great place to watch the weekly Wednesday night sailboat races.

Skyline Drive

Both at night and during the day, a drive along Duluth's Skyline Drive provides breathtaking views of Lake Superior and the city built on the hill. Stop and linger at Hawk's Ridge or pause at Enger Park to climb the stone tower or to ring the Peace Bell, a gift from Duluth's Sister City, Ohara, Japan.

DULUTH'S EAST HILLSIDE
VICTORIAN HOME WITH BEAUTIFUL VIEW

Mathew S. Burrows 1890 Inn

The Mathew S. Burrows 1890 Inn rests on a corner lot in Duluth's East Hillside neighborhood less than a mile from downtown. Surrounded by an ornate wooden fence, the stately Victorian house—with curving and angular architectural lines painted a deep, rich forest green and trimmed in ochre—stands as a dignified, inviting reminder of the town's boom during the latter half of the nineteenth century. Owners Pam and Dave Wolff have worked hard to make the inn a comfortable escape for couples while maintaining Victorian decor in the main floor sitting room and throughout most of its four guest rooms. Deep red plush carpeting leads guests through the entryway and up the stairs to the second floor, and stained glass windows adorn the stairway and other rooms.

The Master Suite at the front of the house features a queen-size carved oak bed, fireplace, and private dressing room. Its bath has a huge claw-foot tub and one of the earliest and most unusual shower systems at any Victorian bed-and-breakfast. Its glass door opens to reveal gleaming, chrome-plated pipes that create a full-body spray—guests often reserve this room specifically because of the bathroom.

The Lakeview Suite at the back of the house takes its name from the vast view of Lake Superior guests enjoy from its sitting room. Its many windows, draped in lace curtains, create the atmosphere of a four-season porch. Lace curtains also drape the room's queen-size four-poster bed. Thick blue carpeting covers the floor, flowered wallpaper hangs on the walls, and an antique nightcap sitting on a bureau completes the room's Victorian charm.

The smaller guest room still offer guests a private bath. The Rose Room's queen-size brass and white iron bed matches the room's wing chairs, while lace panels surround the antique claw-foot tub. The first light of dawn streams through the windows of the intimate Morning Glory Room, which also has a queen-size bed. The beds in each guest room hold a complimentary potpourri sachet that perfumes the room and may be taken home as a memento of the inn.

The dining room's wood inlaid floors, paisley wallpaper, and ornately carved wooden buffet bathe in the light

50 Ways to Lure your Lover

Dress for a buggy ride and take a leisurely sightseeing tour along the waterfront at Canal Park.

of an elaborate stained glass window of Middle Eastern design that almost covers one wall. In the morning, wonderful smells waft out of the kitchen to lead guests to breakfast—fresh-baked breads and muffins, seasonal fruit, coffee, tea, and juice, and a special entree each day—filling enough to last almost until dinner. The Wolffs like to talk to their guests at breakfast time, and encourage guests to get to know one another around the large dining room table.

In the evening the Wolffs turn the first floor over to guests to make them to feel at home, but if needed, Pam and Dave go out of their way to accommodate guests' needs. Once, shortly after the inn opened, a middle-aged couple traveling up the North Shore by motorcycle encountered bad weather while camping at Jay Cooke State Park. They had planned to get married during the trip, but didn't know where or by whom. They showed up at the Burrows Inn dripping wet and in need of a room and a minister. The Wolffs arranged the ceremony, drove the couple to the church, and later toasted the couple with champagne.

Because the Wolffs want the inn to offer couples a romantic retreat from daily pressures, they don't accommodate small children. Call ahead; with only four guest rooms, reservations are recommended, especially on weekends and during the summer and fall months.

1632 E. FIRST ST. • DULUTH

218-724-4991 • 800-789-1890

DULUTH BISTRO

CANAL PARK

Lake Avenue Cafe

wners Tom Benson and Wendy Rouse consider their establishment a cafe, not a restaurant, an attitude reflected in its New York/Parisian bistro-like atmosphere. Exposed duct work and pipes hang from the ceiling of the eatery housed in the beautifully restored and renovated DeWitt-Seitz marketplace. Windows line the two outside walls, adding a bright and airy atmosphere to the L-shaped dining room—the perfect place for couples to relax and enjoy a meal during an afternoon or evening exploring the shops of Canal Park.

Original watercolor paintings by Wendy hang from the walls, and the table decor features an amusing assortment of salt and pepper shakers—a tradition started when, lacking dispensers when the cafe opened, Tom and Wendy used two pink hippos they had picked up in Mexico. The collection has grown over the years through garage sales and donations. Every January during Red Flannel Days in Canal Park, the cafe holds a contest for the best set of salt and pepper shakers. Some of the current sets include a pair of pilgrims, King Kong and the Empire State building, outhouses, chefs, and elephants.

50 Ways
to
Lure your Lover

Send a love letter,

leave a romantic

message on the

answering machine,

or make a date for

lunch by E-mail.

Buy an ad that says

"I love you" in the

local paper.

Tom and Wendy, experienced chefs who have worked and traveled around the world, opened the Lake Avenue Cafe with the goal to serve "good food simply prepared" a definitely understated motto. The food at the Lake Avenue Cafe is excellent; and though they may be simply prepared, many of the menu items such as pesto pizza and eggplant and goat cheese pizza, have an exotic flair. You might begin your meal with the Thai chicken pizza appetizer— a salad-plate-sized treat topped with green onions, carrots, peanuts, chicken, red pepper, garlic, and a touch of ginger and lime. The eclectic menu emphasizes pastas, chicken, seafood, and four entree-size salads with homemade dressings light on oils, with herbs and vinaigrette predominating. Very few red meats are offered.

Save room for desserts, especially the seasonal fresh fruit tortes and a caloric splurge called Chocolate Decadence. They also make delicious cappuccino and have a small but excellent wine list focusing on selections from California vineyards. The beer list includes several local and regional microbrewery selections.

The cafe opens for breakfast at 8:00 A.M. and serves until late in the evening, but is closed on major holidays.

The Lake Avenue Cafe offers "good food simply prepared" —excellent food with an exotic flair.

DEWITT-SEITZ MARKETPLACE

394 LAKE AVENUE SOUTH • CANAL PARK, DULUTH

218-722-2355

HOURS: SUNDAY–THURSDAY, 8:00 A.M.–9:00 P.M.

FRIDAY–SATURDAY, 8:00 A.M.–10:00 P.M.

CANAL PARK, DULUTH

CASUAL DINING IN A LIVELY OLD-TIME ATMOSPHERE

$\mathcal{G}$randma's

 ouples in the northland in search of a fun night out can find it among the many options Grandma's offers in Duluth's Canal Park. Perhaps most famous in Minnesota for its annual marathon, Grandma's has grown from a relatively small operation into a major complex with two branches in the Twin Cities and one in Fargo, North Dakota.

The original Grandma's Saloon and Deli—once a bordello—rests under the shadow of Duluth's famous Aerial Lift Bridge. Antiques of a local theme cover the walls and hang from the rafters, offering a unique glimpse into Duluth's past. The menu features Minnesota fare, including many dishes prepared with wild rice, as well as a selection of sandwiches and the famous monster onion rings.

A renovation during the mid-1980s added Mickey's Grill to the original building. While it shares the bar with the saloon, its kitchen works off a separate menu, focusing on steaks and other grilled delights. Couples wishing a more private dining space should call ahead to reserve

Mickey's Cooler Booth, a separate, intimate dining space that once served as the original restaurant's cooler.

The meals at Grandma's are substantial, so couples may find themselves in need of a way to work off their dinner. While a walk along the nearby Lakewalk is perfect on a warm summer's night, Grandma's offers several active options when the weather is less pleasant. Comedy acts and karaoke entertain guests upstairs in the restaurant's second bar, where the outdoor deck makes a great place to watch ships cruise in and out of the harbor. Below the deck, league members play volleyball throughout the summer, and winter finds the courts iced over for broomball and boot hockey.

And if visitors can't find enough to do at the original Saloon and Deli, a short walk across the parking lot brings them to Grandma's Sports Garden, a nightclub with an emphasis on fun. The huge complex carries the antique theme to the next level, filling every spare space with ancient soda machines, bicycles, and even an airplane. The canopy of an old carousel holds the lighting equipment for the dance floor, and when it is raised, the area becomes an indoor basketball and volleyball court, where leagues play throughout the winter. The Sports Garden also features two bars and several levels—some for video games, others where pizza and burgers

With comedy acts, karaoke, volleyball tournaments, broomball and boot hockey, basketball, and a view of ships entering and leaving the harbor, there is plenty to do and see at Grandma's.

50
Ways
to
Lure your Lover

On a stormy

night, turn off all

the lights, and

cuddle together as

you listen to the

rain on the

windows or

watch the snow

fall silently as the

fire burns softly.

are served—and an entire floor dedicated to pool tables.

Couples staying at any of the nearby hotels can plan their evening around Grandma's—enjoy a hearty meal at the Saloon and Deli, dance it off at the Sports Garden, and take a romantic walk along the canal before returning to their room. And even those who find a long wait at any of the Canal Park locations have yet another option in Duluth—another Grandma's restaurant next to the Miller Hill Mall.

CANAL PARK • DULUTH

218-727-4192

HOURS: MONDAY–SUNDAY, 11:00 A.M.–11:00 P.M.

DULUTH

ENGLISH PUB WITH LIVE MUSIC JAM SESSIONS

Sir Benedict's

One wouldn't expect to find an English pub along Minnesota's North Shore, but Sir Benedict's at the head of the lake offers a cozy retreat for visitors to sample a large collection of imported beers and ales or grab a light meal.

In the winter, Sir Benedict's makes a warm sanctuary when cold winter winds blow off icy Lake Superior. In the warm months, however, guests of the pub enjoy their food and drink outside on the front patio, where tables bloom with bright umbrellas, providing the atmosphere of a northern-European open-air cafe. The cold winds of winter become cooling breezes that push away the humidity of summer, providing natural air conditioning.

Sir Benedict's serves thick, tasty sandwiches that start with one of three fresh-baked, wholesome breads, which are topped with a choice of three or four varieties of meat and cheese and several different toppings, including a rich guacamole. During cold nights in January and February, homemade soups, including a wonderful French onion,

50
Ways
to
Lure your Lover

Stroll through the

Rose Garden

along Duluth's

boardwalk,

stopping for

coffee or wine at

a spot with a

patio that over-

looks the lake.

turn an evening's visit to the pub into a delicious retreat from the cold. The soups—and everything else on the menu—are served year round. For those whose taste doesn't run toward beer, the pub also offers a variety of nonalcoholic juices, sodas, seltzers, tea, and coffee.

Wednesday nights Sir Ben's comes alive with music, juxtaposing the pub's British atmosphere with very American sounds of bluegrass. Musicians from in and around the Twin Ports area join in the informal setting to play for whoever stops in. Everyone is welcome to join in or simply relax with a date over an imported beer, letting the music and laughter punctuate the romance.

805 EAST SUPERIOR ST. • DULUTH

218-728-1192

HOURS: MONDAY, TUESDAY, AND SATURDAY, 11:00 A.M.–MIDNIGHT

WEDNESDAY–FRIDAY, 11:00 A.M.–12:30 A.M.

SUNDAY, 11:00 A.M.–10:00 P.M.

Hacienda Del Sol

Visitors to Duluth may not expect to find traditional Mexican food this close to the Canadian border, but residents know where to enjoy a southwestern treat in the heart of the Northland. The Hacienda Del Sol offers a cozy spot for a couple to share a spicy meal on the eastern edge of downtown Duluth.

The tiny restaurant—with its wooden booths, countertop dining, and semi-exposed kitchen—has the old-fashioned feel of a 1940s eatery, but its decor gives it the charm of a Mexican cafe. An Aztec/Mayan theme runs through the wall hangings, while cacti and other desert flora fill the large bay windows on either side of the entrance, creating a quick escape south of the border during the cold of a northland winter.

During summer months, guests find the same on a mural covering the high walls that enclose the restaurant's bi-level courtyard. Trees shade parts of the courtyard, which opens sometime after the ice breaks up on Lake Superior and closes right around the first frost, creating a wonderful spot for couples to enjoy a meal and each other's company on warm summer nights.

Made from recipes owner Kevin Deutsch developed from his experience as a cook in East Los Angeles, the Mexican food at Hacienda Del Sol has a flair all its own. Kevin started with traditional recipes, then adapted them, adding a combination of flavors from various regions of Mexico. The restaurant prepares everything on site, including its own tortilla shells and chips. The menu features a traditional offering of burritos, tacos, and enchiladas served ala carte or with rice and refried beans topped with cheese. All are available with beef or chicken, but adventurous diners will want to try theirs with chorizo, a special Mexican sausage. The restaurant also serves unique chiles rellenos, and, for the faint of palate, their famous grilled peanut butter and jelly sandwich.

The restaurant prepares everything on site, including its own tortilla shells and chips. And the hot sauce here is truly hot.

Many appetizers—including a delicious quesadilla and a killer plate of nachos—grace the menu, and all items can be prepared using the restaurant's own mild, medium, or hot sauces. The hot sauce here is truly hot, yet it retains a distinct taste—not just heat. Kevin uses jalepeños and a variety of other chiles to create a green sauce guaranteed to make even the heartiest diners' eyes water.

The Hacienda Del Sol also serves a wide variety of

Mexican and domestic beers, wine, coffee, tea, and soft drinks—including a wonderful cherry-vanilla creme soda, an interesting accompaniment to mexican cuisine.

Saying "I love you"

SPANISH

Te amo

319 E. SUPERIOR STREET • DULUTH

218-722-7296

MONDAY–THURSDAY, 11:00 A.M.–11:00 P.M.

FRIDAY–SATURDAY, 11:00 A.M.–12:00 MIDNIGHT

CLOSED SUNDAYS

WINTER HOURS: MONDAY–THURSDAY, 11:00 A.M.–10:00 P.M.

DOWNTOWN DULUTH

AUTHENTIC GREEK CUISINE, MUSIC, BELLY DANCING

Natchio's Greektown

lack-and-white photos of Greek weddings greet diners as they enter Natchio's Greektown, a romantic little restaurant tucked along the bricked streets of downtown Duluth. The food and atmosphere at Natchio's remind diners that Duluth is an international port. The folks at Natchio's understand the vital link between good eating and the good life, and that philosophy (from the Greek for "love of wisdom") turns an evening out into a celebration.

A small dining area sits to the left of the restaurant's entrance, its tall windows flooding the room with light during the afternoon and reflecting it at night. To the right, two levels of dining space dotted with tables for two or four await diners. Large black-and-white photos of Greece and a Greek flag decorate the exposed walls of the upper level, and traditional music of the Mediterranean fills the rooms. On Saturday nights, they turn the music up a notch as a belly dancer entertains diners.

The cuisine celebrates the owners' Greek heritage.

Start the evening off with an olive, pepper, or feta cheese appetizer, or try the calamari, spanakopita or the Greektown Mesé, a super hors d'oeuvre tray for two. Traditional Greek entrees range from moussaka, thick slices of eggplant with a layer of meat, tomato, and wine sauce topped by a cheese custard, to dolmathes, delicately seasoned ground beef with rice wrapped in grape leaves and bathed in hollandaise sauce. Those who can't make up their minds might try the Greek Feast, a combination of hors d'oeuvres, soup and salad, and a choice of entree served with manestra, Greek potato, and moussaka. The feast even includes coffee and baklava. Natchio's also serves lighter fare for those not ready to tackle a full meal, including traditional offerings such as taxoes, agora, of course, and stefato, a wonderful shepherd's stew of beef and onions simmered in wine.

50
Ways
to
Lure your Lover

Meet for lunch at

a restaurant with

an international

flair. Bring

flowers.

No visit to a Greek restaurant would be complete without coffee and dessert. Natchio's brews a special Greek blend to accompany their baklava, kourabethis, and theeplis. Natchio's menu reminds us that the ancient Greeks believed that philosophy (the love of wisdom) was best when practiced at a symposium, which originally meant "drinking party," where artists and philosophers gathered to toast each others' health. Modern-day romantics can toast romantic love at Natchio's with

one of the menu's fine assortment of Greek wines or a cock-
tail or beer. No matter what you choose to eat and drink at
Natchio's, its staff will ensure your evening out turns into
a celebration.

109 NORTH SECOND AVENUE WEST • DULUTH

218-722-6585

HOURS: MONDAY–FRIDAY, 11:00 A.M.–9:00 P.M.

SATURDAY, 12:00 NOON–10:00 P.M.

CLOSED ON SUNDAYS

DOWNTOWN DULUTH

REVOLVING RESTAURANT FEATURING MINNESOTA FARE

Top of the Harbor

In a city known for its views, what could be better than to take it all in—the city, the harbor, the rows of houses seemingly stacked on top of one another—while enjoying a fine meal.

At the Top of the Harbor, a classic revolving restaurant found on the sixteenth floor of the Radisson Hotel at downtown Duluth's western edge, diners sit at tables on a carousel that slowly rotates. Surrounded by large windows, the moving dining room provides a panoramic—and quite romantic—view of the residential neighborhoods above the hotel as well as downtown, the harbor, and Duluth's famous Aerial Lift Bridge connecting Minnesota Point to Canal Park. Couples enjoying an evening meal find themselves entertained by the ever-changing view of Duluth's city lights and those of the ships and sailboats dotting the harbor below.

The cuisine at the Top of the Harbor is as wonderful as the view. The menu has a decidedly Minnesota theme, including entrees such as roast Minnesota duck breast,

173

Served at a table dressed in candlelight and surrounded by the lights of Duluth, the Chateau Briand for Two makes a wonderful choice for a romantic meal at the head of the greatest Great Lake.

broiled or pan-fried Minnesota walleyed pike, broiled Lake Superior trout, and the Lake Superior Sampler, which combines broiled salmon, lake trout, and walleye. Diners can select Minnesota wild rice to accompany any of their dinner selections.

Other choices include a wonderful selection of steaks, roast pork loin medallions, and chicken Oscar, a sauteed chicken breast with crab meat and asparagus covered in bérnaise sauce. Besides fresh Lake Superior fish, seafood such as Alaskan salmon, cold water lobster, and jumbo Gulf shrimp are also available, as is the Shrimp ala Radisson, shrimp sauteed with a blend of scallions, artichoke hearts, white wine, and just a hint of garlic.

The restaurant's kitchen has also developed a special meal just for couples, the Chateau Briand for Two. This feast includes a sixteen ounce choice filet mignon carved at the table and served with vegetables, oven-browned red potatoes, and sauteed mushrooms and complemented with two glasses of cabernet sauvignon. Served at a table dressed in candlelight and surrounded by the lights of Duluth, the Chateau Briand for Two makes a wonderful choice for a romantic meal at the head of the greatest Great Lake.

RADISSON HOTEL • 505 W. SUPERIOR ST. • DULUTH
218-727-8981 • 800-333-3333 • RESERVATIONS RECOMMENDED
OPEN SEVEN DAYS A WEEK 6:30 A.M.–10:00 P.M.

Pfeifer-Hamilton Publishers produces quality gift books celebrating the special beauty and unique lifestyle of the north country.

by Shawn Perich
Fishing Lake Superior
The North Shore

by Scott Anderson
Distant Fires

by Nadine and Craig Blacklock
Gooseberry

by Bob Cary
Root Beer Lady

by Sam Cook
Up North
Quiet Magic
CampSights

by Laura Erickson
For the Birds

by Michael Furtman
Canoe Country Camping

by Mark Stensaas
Canoe Country Wildlife

by Jerry Wilber
Wit and Wisdom of the Great Outdoors

by Douglas Wood
Paddle Whispers

Call us toll free at 800-247-6789 for a complete catalog.

Pfeifer-Hamilton Publishers
210 West Michigan Duluth MN 55802-1908